The Calico Shaman

True Tales of Animal Communication

By Carla Person with Hillary Johnson

COCCORA PRESS
VENETA, OREGON

Published by Coccora Press, P.O. Box 697, Veneta, OR 97487
541.935.4996

Cover Design and Book Layout by Don Person

Illustrations by Ken Hooper

ISBN 0-9744145-0-6

To my spirit teachers for their eternal love

Table of Contents

Prologue
All of These Stories Are True

Whatever tribe you come from, you have a tradition of healing stories that are passed from one generation to the next, retold around campfires, on stages or in books. All tribes have stories to tell, and it turns out that all species do, too. Collected in this book are some of the stories Carla Person has been told by assorted cats, dogs and horses while working as a shamanic animal healer.

Each of the stories in this book is based on the transcripts from one of Carla's healing sessions. Typically, Carla begins a session knowing only the animal's name, age, gender and breed, and the nature of the health or behavior problem to be solved. Sometimes, but not always, the animal's owner has sent along a photograph, but since Carla's clients live all over the globe, she almost never meets them in the flesh.

As the session begins, Carla closes her eyes and uses the beat of her drum to enter a trance state, journeying into that primordial dreamspace common to seers of all cultures. Like Oz or Neverland, Carla's shamanic world has its own magical geography. It also has its own logic: for one thing, time and space do not behave themselves in any orderly fashion. Pigs can fly here, for example - and they often do.

You will meet lots of creatures in these pages, from wizards to worms, but the cast of central characters remains the same. Carla's friends in the spirit world have kindly agreed to participate in the writing of this book. In the very first tale you will meet Amber, a Scottish redhead who can be counted on to know just the right potion or procedure whenever there's a cat in crisis. Then there's Kay, a lanky Native-American healer whose bachelor pad digs are a bit gamy, even though his corrals are spotless. Kay has a way with dogs, and his horse, an Appaloosa named Star Spangled Banner, steps in to help with most equine complaints.

All shamans are keepers of information that is sacred. The nature of a shaman's power animals — those mystical beings who arrive when summoned to help in performing healing rituals — is often a closely-held secret. Accordingly, the identities of Carla's power animals have been changed out of respect for their real-life counterparts' spiritual modesty. Be aware that when you encounter an osprey, a wolverine, or a Caribou working alongside Carla, these animals are standing in for shyer species.

In no other instance, however, does this text deviate from the transcripts of Carla's journeys. As you read, you can rest assured that those crusty comebacks from the chief of the Maine Coon tribe are coming to you verbatim, and that Aria is a real cat who lives in Northern California with her owner, Ellen.

Some stories only get truer in the retelling. In fleshing out the details of what began as individual healing sessions, the stories came alive in entirely new ways. What the animals had to say turned out to be as universal as the teachings that we all know come out of the mouths of babes. In short, the stories went from being merely real, to being true. And as you read them, they will become truer still.

— *Hillary Johnson*

Introduction

How a toy company marketing executive became a shamanic animal healer

I am a tree; a trunk grown from spirit *graced with branches from the sky. My roots stretch into the Lower World, filled with the blood of life itself. As I work, the tree leafs out and fills with beauty. When I teach, it fills with fruits. Through the gentle initiation of experience, the seeds ripen, each one imprinted with its own experience. As they take root and stretch skyward, each new sapling offers its own flourish to the diverse forest. Attracted by the intoxicating power of compassion, the spirits come, the animals come and the forest spirit nurtures all who enter.*

I am a shamanic healer, and this is my business plan.

I came into shamanic work through a healing. In my mid-twenties, my sister recommended that I visit a woman in Santa Fe named Sandra Ingerman. She was researching a shamanic healing technique called "soul retrieval," and my sister thought she could help me come to grips with my childhood. It wasn't that I was struggling with childhood issues — I simply didn't remember large chunks of time.

The session was astounding. Sandra asked me to lie down, then she sang a song and shook her rattle.

Finally, she lay down next to me with a drumming tape on her headphones. After a time, we sat up. She cupped her hands and blew into the top of my head and into my chest. It felt like a windstorm coming through. She brought back three parts of myself that had separated during traumatic moments, and then, in what felt to me like the ultimate coming home, she blew in the spirit of a black horse: my first power animal.

We talked about what she had learned from these soul parts — why they left, what gifts they could bring me now — and she gave me pointers on helping them to reintegrate. (Over time, these parts did bring back rich memories, some benign and some that helped me really understand who I am.)

Then she said the words that changed my life: "The spirits have told me you have psychic ability and it would be good for you to get training. I recommend that you take the basic workshop with the Foundation for Shamanic Studies."

I knew she was right, but I have to say that I had directed my life in quite the other direction. I was working as a marketing manager at Kenner Toys, deeply involved in the creation and selling of boys' action figures, like Super Powers and Batman. But at the same time I knew my spirit had other roots. In high school I studied mystical things like the Kabbala and the I Ching. In college I devoted myself to the great books, and struggled to understand the world's deepest mysteries. But I couldn't make a living as a philosopher, so I joined the ranks and got an MBA, which quickly immersed me in 60-hour weeks of deadlines and meetings. Sandra's words motivated me. I signed up for the next workshop in my area.

The basic workshop introduced me to the idea of shamanism, and for several years I slowly developed my skills, working with different people, reading and taking workshops, but still immersed in a work-driven world. Then, in 1993, the spirits sent me a vision and the means to fulfill it. A recruiter asked me to join a software firm in Eugene, Oregon. When I asked the spirits about it, they gave me a strong vision of a group of ancient women — my spiritual sisters — and said I would find them. They then showed me a vintage building in Eugene filled with bookish programmers who hung out at the WOW dance hall after work. The images became reality.

My stint at the software company was very short and miserable. While it didn't feel like a blessing at the time, the pain I suffered required intensive healing work, and that work drove me deep into the arms of the compassionate spirits. I spent several months recovering, studying wild mushrooms and listening to the spirits for guidance. They showed me the image of a felled redwood tree with multiple sprouts surging from its stump. They helped me meet my spiritual sisters. They filled my mind with creative projects and ideas.

But then, like a classic "hero," I refused the calling and tried to jump back into the corporate stream. I took a job in San Francisco and commuted by airplane from Eugene, trying to keep a foot in both worlds. That job was incredibly comfortable, but I knew after a few months that it wasn't right for me. I simply had to answer the call. My new boss was incredulous. He even offered me a bright red Porsche 911 if I stayed. But I had to go. I took a job as an adjunct instructor of marketing at the University of Oregon. And I got serious about my shamanic work.

My human-based training comes largely from workshops I have done with exceptional native and modern shamanic practitioners. The most meaningful training, however, comes directly from the spirits themselves. About halfway through the Foundation for Shamanic Studies three-year advanced

13

training program, I made the decision to hang out my shingle and share this work professionally, but I wasn't really sure how to go about it. Many of my colleagues were therapists or otherwise experienced in helping people with their troubles. I had never even taken a psychology class. All I knew about was consumer product marketing...and *working with horses*!

During those years, on a parallel path, I was learning to communicate with horses through body language and emotional connection. Like most long-time horse people, I was taught as a child to dominate the horse, and I had all sorts of bad habits to unlearn. My budding herd of Icelandics was helping me as I discovered new ways of connecting and teaching. In many ways, it was like a shamanic journey. Learning the gentle training and touch system called TTEAM with Robyn Hood and the quintessential positive reinforcement method of clicker training with Alexander Kurland, I centered myself in gentleness to connect with the horse, then guided the results through positive intention and compassion. After a consultation with my Spirit Teachers, I decided to devote my work to healing animals. It didn't take much reflection to realize that my life is all about animals. In addition to our five horses, my husband, Don, and I currently share life with ten cats and two dogs, plus plenty of chickens, fish and wildlife. It was no stretch at all to begin applying the shamanic healing techniques I had learned to animal clients. My spiritual teachers were happy to help.

When I am doing shamanic healing work, I go deep into a trance-like state, where I work with my spirit teachers to diagnose and heal the spiritual aspects of the client's troubles. If the client is suffering a chronic pain, I may see a spiritual intrusion in that place, and work to remove it. Or I may find that part of the client's soul has gone missing as a result of

14

abuse or trauma, in which case I will retrieve that soul part and bring it back home where it belongs. Many troublesome things in "Ordinary Reality" have spiritual counterparts, and healing that spiritual aspect in "Non-Ordinary Reality" often results in profound physical and behavioral changes.

When I do my work, I set my intention for my session, and I work intensely with the spirit teachers to get to the bottom of the problems and fix them. First, I meet the animal on a spiritual level, introducing myself and gaining their permission to work with them. If the animal's person has everyday sorts of questions such as "What is your favorite food?" I will often ask these at this point, before I begin the shamanic healing work, because the animal is still close to his normal way of being. Often, animals are too mellow at the end of a session to care much about answering mundane questions. After that, I dive into shamanic work, congressing with magical images and the gifts of the spirits to diagnose and heal all sorts of traumas and troubles. No two sessions are ever alike, and every aspect of the session is healing for the animal and guardian. People often listen to the recordings I send over and over again, playing them for the animal as well.

When I began my practice, it was challenging for me to perform simple communication tasks, because I had learned to quickly enter a very deep state, far past the point at which telepathic animal communication commonly occurs. But as I learned to pause at the gateway to deep work, and converse with the animal at that place, I realized that the shamanic method is ideal for animal communication. The key is to keep it simple and clear. In my workshops, I teach a streamlined method of shamanic journeying entirely focused on communicating with animals. The students travel to a favorite Middle World nature spot and learn to shift consciousness.

Then they connect with a personal power animal, and seek its wisdom and advice. When they become adept at moving into their Middle World spot and meeting their power animal, we introduce a client animal. The power animal brings the client animal's spirit to the person, and the communication flows like water. Complete beginners often get profound and verifiable information their first time!

During the second day, we focus on helping clients gain information helpful to resolving an issue an animal is experiencing. It can be an emotional concern, physical trouble or a behavior problem. The students learn why the animal believes the problem is occurring and what can be done about it. The information is often quite significant and helpful to the guardian.

Then I ask them to ask the power animals opinions about the problem, and to get the power animal's advice on how to alleviate it. Bang! The information is richer, deeper and far more profound. We are beginning to shift from using the shamanic journey to facilitate animal communication into actually practicing shamanism. This is where the doors blow wide open. This is where people begin to move outside of themselves, outside of their egos. They realize that they are bringing knowledge that is profound for both the animal and human. They are reaching into the sublime.

Shamans were probably the original animal communicators. They spoke with the animals to gain information for hunting and many other useful things. Today, we commonly think of telepathy when we think of interspecies communication. Telepathic communicators exchange images, feeling, thoughts and ideas with the spiritual mind of other beings. Sometimes this is referred to as a "mind to mind connection." In many ways, it is similar to the shamanic method. Just as in shamanic journeying, the keys to success in telepathic work are focus, intention and aligning one's heart with the power of compassion.

But Shamanic animal communication differs from telepathic in two key respects: The first is the use of the shamanic journey to enter Non-Ordinary Reality, where we meet the client animal's spirit—often as clearly as though we were sitting next to him in the room. This time-honored technique takes the communicator to a deep level very quickly, and the experience of Non-Ordinary Reality adds richness and meaning that may otherwise not be present in telepathic work. Second, and most importantly, in shamanic animal communication we always work in conjunction with our spirit allies. These wise and compassionate beings connect us to the client animal, and add valuable information that, often, the client animal can't even begin to describe. And they protect us from any hazards we may encounter in our work.

It's hard to put a finger on exactly what happens in a shamanic journey. Sometimes the images and messages are clear and direct, as if experiencing the animal in Ordinary Reality. Sometimes, however, the messages are obtuse and metaphorical, and require interpretation or just plain faith that the spirits have properly addressed the issues.

A session I did for Chongo, an adorable, small mixed-breed dog, offers a simple example of the additional information that the spirits can bring. Chongo told me that his right rear foot occasionally stung, causing him to limp, and that the hip hurt sometimes as well. His mistress confirmed that the dog does indeed occasionally limp, on the rear leg; she had thought he had something stuck in his paw. Chongo could give me no explanation as to how he came to hurt at all, except to show me a funhouse mirror of multiple images of himself, as though he were everywhere at once and playing hard. My spirit teacher explained that, as a pup, Chongo had been bitten in the hip and foot in play with his siblings. Those sharp puppy teeth! The hip bite had infected slightly, causing a boil-like wound. The boil healed, but the memory of the event remained in the form of an intrusion. We extracted it, put in some healing power and Chongo was delighted!

It all depends upon how deeply into the journey state one has gone. To help me explain this, the Spirits have graciously provided a model that tells a likely story of how spiritual communication works (much like Plato told a likely story that reality is actually the dancing of shadows on the cave wall). It goes like this:

Most spiritual traditions tell us that in some mysterious way we are "all one." It is as though there were a continuum from our individual selves in Ordinary Reality to our connected selves in Non-Ordinary Reality. In the shamanic journey, we are walking out along that continuum, traveling out into our more connected selves, to join with the selves of other beings, such as our animal clients and the blessed Spirit teachers. I find that the animal communication aspects of my work occurs on a part of the continuum that is closer to the individual self, and the intense healing work often occurs farther out on the continuum, sometimes at a very deep level where individual selves are indistinct. Negotiating this continuum is a core skill in my work.

Shamanic healing typically addresses the spiritual aspect of a problem, and is often the wind in the sails that allows complete recovery. While I can never make the promise, sometimes the spirits do grant obvious and miraculous healings. Most often, however, shamanic healing is part of a team effort including the guardian, veterinarians, naturopaths, massage therapists, chiropractors, Reiki masters and so forth. It can be hard to pinpoint cause and effect, but I can promise that the spirits who agree to intercede on behalf of an animal will do their best. Sometimes their effort brings a vision or understanding to a team member, who then knows exactly what to do. And sometimes their efforts facilitate the natural healing process, enabling the immune system to win. But sometimes they just plain fix it. Like they did with a little kitten in Eugene.

I was asked to help a three-week-old kitten who had a bizarre deformity. Her rear legs didn't connect into the hip sockets correctly, and she moved more like frog than a cat. She wasn't in pain, and she was active, but the guardians were concerned about her ongoing quality of life. I held the kitten, and journeyed to my teacher Amber, who helps cats. She merged with me and sent healing power into the kitten. In this case, I didn't sense any intrusion, power loss or soul loss—just that the kitten needed a healing power boost. The power felt warm coming through me, and I trembled slightly as the power moved from Amber through my hands. It was only for a moment, but it did the job. Ten days later, the guardian called to say the kitten had rapidly progressed and was then completely normal. Thank you, spirits!

As you will soon see, I work with several human spirit teachers and a host of animal spirits. They each have talents, and some prefer to work with one particular species. All were once alive on this planet and understand the pain and suffering we undergo. Their purpose in joining with me is to relieve that suffering. Virtually all of my work is done at a distance, and my clients are all over the globe.

The usual course of my work is to first gather information from the person — the name and description of the animal, the issues that brought them to me and any specific information they wish to learn and/or share with the animal. I then wire myself with a microphone connected to a CD recorder, and I drum to call in the spirits and begin my journey. Once I am in Non-Ordinary Reality, I beseech my spirits to help. We then go to the animal's spirit, gain its permission to help, and begin the diagnostic and healing work. I translate my experiences into words and speak aloud, recording the session onto a CD so that the guardian can experience it as well and get the direct benefit of the spirits' healing words and songs. My sessions usually run 30 to 40 minutes but have taken as long as an hour and a half.

The stories here are taken from transcripts of these sessions, enriched with Hillary Johnson's magical skills. Hillary is versed in shamanism, and has journeyed to my teachers to have them fill in the little details that I may have forgotten to mention as I did the session, such as her rich descriptions of the Upper World and Amber's home. Like all messages from spirit, these words are filled with healing power. So as you read them, bask in the compassionate love of the spirits, for the animals, their guardians, and for you.

– Carla Person

The Characters and their Spirit Homeland

These stories take place in the Upper, Middle and Lower Worlds of Non-Ordinary Reality. Most shamanic cultures recognize these three basic distinctions of place. Shamans enter these lands by going into a trance-like state, where they can experience these worlds as vividly as we see our everyday world of Ordinary Reality. Some cultures focus their work in one place or another.

The Middle World is the non-ordinary, spiritual dimension of Ordinary Reality. When we connect with the spirits of trees, mountains and such, we are generally connecting with their Middle World spiritual selves. The Upper World lies above a cloud barrier, high above us. To get there, a person first journeys to their Middle World place in nature, then sets the intention to go to the Upper World. After crossing through a thin barrier, typically of clouds or a translucent membrane, most people see the Upper World as a beautiful land filled with light, crystals and heavenly images. I find my teacher, Amber, there. She helps me with cats and personal issues. I also have a teacher there who helps me plan my garden — handy!

The Lower World is accessed through a tunnel or a waterway. After burrowing down for some time, the journeyer comes to a bright light, the entrance to the Lower World. There, they usually find a land that looks much like earth, filled with plants and animal spirits. While it is most typical to see human spirits in the Upper World and animal spirits in the lower, there are human spirits, and spirits of all descriptions in all three lands.

These stories take place in all three worlds. I begin by entering the Middle World and settling myself into my favorite spot in the Arizona desert. From there I travel skyward, to the Upper World to visit Amber, a beautiful Scottish lady, or down through an animal burrow into the Lower World to visit Kay, a striking Native American man and the horse who shares his home, Star Spangled Banner. These teachers have been working closely with me for years and have specialties. Amber loves cats and is my first line of wisdom for anything feline. Kay is a horseman who can address any issue from lameness to training. He even gives me riding lessons when I visit on my own time. I've journeyed to them to interview them for this book, so they can introduce themselves to you in their own words.

Interview with Amber

Carla: Amber, I have come to ask you if you would like a to say a few words at the beginning of the book.

Amber: Certainly. Here is what I have to say. I was born in the Scottish Highlands in 1638. I was a small girl raised with sheep. Sometimes I looked like a sheep because my hair was as unwieldy as a sheep's. I learned all of the womanly arts and had quite a few suitors. That time when I was young and free was the favorite time of my life, the part I have shown you most often. But there were other times after that that were harder. After I was married we went through a hard winter where we lost virtually everything. There was a Wee One (a spirit being) who would bring me food to feed the family. Grain would appear on my shelf when we needed it. I made offerings to him, and gave thanks, and he would take them. Little things my husband wouldn't miss would disappear. One day I lost my husband too, and then I was alone. A man came on a horse and said I have a book for you. But I did not know how to read. He read it to me. It was *Workings of Wisdoms* and it was filled with messages for me. My children had grown so I decided to follow the path this book laid out for me. I left my country home and went to town. There was a woman older than me there, and I moved in with her. She and I did chores together. And she taught me the old ways. She could speak to the cats and she would tell me everything that was going on around town from the cats. We became known as the cat ladies. When cats were hurt and the little girls who loved them would bring them to us, my friend would heal them. And by and by I learned how to heal them too using the old ways.

I won't trouble you with how I died, it doesn't matter. But my children did mourn me and they put a cat's statue on my grave. And this is why cats and I are so close. And I am happy to help you with them my dear.

Carla: Anything else?

Amber: Be sure to say I was always beautiful!

Interview with Star Spangled Banner (Kay's Appaloosa companion.)

My spots came from the stars reflecting upon me. My hooves are flint and my mane is fire. I am no ordinary being and I never have been one. I am an idea born into the horses connected to my friend Kay. No matter whatever, when he rides a horse in any lifetime, he always rides me.

Interview with Kay

Kay: I have lived many lifetime with horses. And in-between them I live with horses too. Horses are as much a part of me as my hair. I am sure that my soul has existed before horses and will exist after horses, but it is my time with horses that is most interesting to me. I've been born in California, Montana and Missouri. My ancestors were from Alaska and Northern Canada. We are Siberians. And I have lived lives back there too, but what interests me most are the lifetimes lived with the horses which is why I tell you about the times I lived in your North America with horses.

Carla: Were you not with horses in Siberia? They are famous for horses.

Kay: Maybe I was, but this is not what I show you when I work with you. Any spirit can be all things. Now let us have some coffee and smoked salmon. I am so glad you moved to the Pacific Northwest where the food is so good. And maybe the only thing as good as horses is food.

Carla: I do agree. I love good food.

Kay: I know you do. That's why we get along so well.

Thank you spirits for sharing a bit of your stories with us.

Finally I want to say a word about why we chose to write these stories in third person. Shamanic journeys are bigger than we are. When we enter Non-Ordinary Reality and connect with spirits, they speak to us on many levels at once, giving immediate information and action regarding the intention of the journey, and opening the doorways to the Universe's deepest, richest mysteries. Just as Kay says that every spirit can be all things, so every journey has universal wisdom that may go far deeper than the story's obvious flow. By telling these stories in third person we are hoping to make it easier for each reader to access the wisdom that is right for them, for their own healing and knowledge. The character *Carla* is really just another vector for the spirits to bless you, dear reader, with what you need. My personal ego steps aside, making it easier for you to step in.

Grandmother, can you tell me a story to guide us?

This story was given to me word for word by an ancient Grandmother Spirit who helps me in my journeys. Her wisdom and healing power have touched many animals and humans who have sought her help. I asked her to share a healing story to set the stage, and to help us write powerful words and to help you, gentle reader, be receptive to the healing and revelations in the stories that follow.

– Carla

Healing is an art form, child, a gift from the spirits, to the spirits, and sifted down from the sky. It takes many hours to prepare for a great healing, great care in each detail to please the ancestors, to please the spirits, to please the great ones who love us and come from so far to heed our call. The great robes of the shamans are woven with the details of each minute aspect of their preparation. The preparation goes back generations, and your lifetime is but one of many generations of your own preparation. Never dismiss the importance of that preparation; emphasize it. Make sure the importance of the preparation is deeply embedded into your work.

This is the story of Little Cornflower.

Mother is making tortillas, and Little Cornflower asks, "How may I help?"

"Oh, Little Cornflower, you can certainly help! You can help by going out and asking the weeds to leave the ground."

So Little Cornflower runs out. "Weeds, leave! Weeds, leave!" she yells over the patch of ground where the corn will grow. Her mother smiles.

"I've asked them to leave, Mother. Now how can I help?"

"Little Cornflower, you can help by traveling across the mountains to Uncle's to get the seed."

Little Cornflower straps the sack on her back, and she flies across the mountains. The journey takes her three days. While at Uncle's, she is given much food and refreshment, and a full sack of seeds. On her way home she gets lost.

"Now what will I do?"

Crow calls to her from behind: "I might be able to help."

He shows her the way in exchange, of course, for seeds. She shares her seed with Crow, and when she returns, she has not a sack-full, but a handful.

"Oh, little child, you have learned how important the preparations are, and how easy it is to get off track," her Mother says, "but a handful will begin."

"Now how can I help?"

"Take your handful of corn seeds and go out and scratch them into the ground."

So Little Cornflower does, and as she scratches them into the ground she sees the squirrels watching. "Oh, no squirrels! No, no squirrels! If you do not eat my seed, I will promise to share the ears with you."

28

The squirrels say, "That is an even trade. We like you, Little Cornflower."

She ruffles her skirts and goes back inside, and tells her mother the compromise she has made with the squirrels. Her mother is pleased. But she says, "Do you trust them?"

"How can I not trust them, Mother?"

"Then trust them indeed."

Little Cornflower runs back outside just to make sure, and the squirrels indeed are worrying about nuts, and burying them, and leaving her corn patch entirely alone.

"Oh, Mother, how can I help now?" she says again.

"Your corn must be watered. You must dance for rain."

Little Cornflower is not sure how to do that. But she goes next door to her Auntie's, who is a great rain dancer. Auntie sews her the skirt that she needs, and the beaded top, and gives her the wands for her hands, and shows her how to make the moves.

For an entire week, Little Cornflower learns how to dance for rain, and then she is ready. She goes out. The ground is very dry. She says, "I am just in time," and she dances for rain. She dances hard for rain. She dances all night for rain, and in the morning she hears the crack of thunder, and it pours down on her cornfield.

The crow who showed her the way comes, and he says, "You are doing a good job, Little Cornflower. And for sharing your corn with me, I will protect your crop."

She looks at him and says, "That is odd. I was supposed to protect the crop from you."

The crow replies, "You make good preparations. And when you make good preparations, your enemy becomes your friend."

Little Cornflower says, "I do not understand you, but I believe you."

And her belief in what she sees becomes her marker. It becomes her way. As she grew to be an old seer, she would say, "I believe what I see. And it is so." And no one would deny her.

Little Cornflower's crop grew strong and mighty, with extra ears on each of the few stalks. She shared ears with the squirrels, and they showed her how to bury them. They planted her next year's crop. Crow came to be Cornflower's spirit guide teacher. And when she was an old woman and could no longer see, Crow saw for her, and she believed him.

That is the story for the beginning of your book.

You want my kitty, don't you?

Timmy and the Ladies of the Club

Have you ever heard of a storytelling cat? Of course you have. Every time a cat blinks or flicks its ears at you, it's daring you to believe some fancy tail or other. Cats were put on this earth—well, the exact reasons are confidential—but one of the reasons is to unravel the yarns that we humans wrap into tight little balls. That long, stringy tangle that is your life—your cat may be there to help you unravel it. Of course, not all cats are pros, and yours may just be passing through for the free kip and kibble, or to soak up that irresistible sunbeam that falls on the Oriental rug in your dining room every afternoon, but some cats do seek out their people for a reason.

When Timmy the big grey street cat wandered into Debra's life, he seemed so determined and assured, so very much in charge, that she called me in to settle once and for all just who was there to look after who.

Deb was one of my first clients. She is a great cat lover, and quite a talented animal communicator herself. When Timmy came to her, she knew he was special, in part because he is drop dead gorgeous, but mostly because he carried himself with an unmistakable sense of purpose.

"Carla," Deb wrote in an email, "this cat Timmy is very much an enigma. I don't know where he came from. He showed up at my office, and now he's part of my household, but I just don't know what to make of him."

"Street cats can be imperious, and moody — oh yes!" replied Carla. "It seems to be something in the tribe. But I will journey on it, and ask my friend Amber what she thinks. If Timmy is with you for a reason, Amber will get to the bottom of it.

Carla logged off the computer in the second-floor office space at the back of her farmhouse. A white, airy room with an improbable electric blue carpet, it overlooked the paddock where her three Icelandic horses, Jark, Elmar and Kolur, grazed beside the seasonal goldfish pond built and stocked by her husband, Don.

Carla spread the tools of her trade out on the bright blue carpet and went to work while two black Labs dozed by the patio door along with two or three of the ten cats who frequented the farm house. Her kit was simple:

- A rattle
- A hoop drum made of maple and elk hide
- A sachet of herbs that, when squeezed, let off a cleansing whiff of dust
- A tape recorder
- A velvet bag full of polished stones
- Another bag containing some bright green feathers voluntarily shed by a tropical bird

And, in each of the room's four corners, a picture representing a different view of the place where she was about to go.

But most of Carla's tools were quite invisible to the naked eye.

Sitting still with her legs crossed, Carla began to beat her drum in a steady rhythm. At first, the sound danced in syncopation with her breath and the tom-tom of her heart, and soon her whole being began to play along with the steady waves rising out of the wood and elk hide. The universe has a rhythm. All travel is a matter of synching up. There's the rhythm of walking, the rhythm of running, the rhythm of riding, and the rhythms of desire, dreaming and fear; and then there's this: the rhythm of the shaman's path, a beat that causes the three-dimensional world to shimmer away, revealing the shapes and colors of Non-Ordinary realms.

Her eyes closed, Carla left the small white room in the uppermost corner of the farmhouse and rose through the air, flying now, to her Middle World place where she settled into a pool of soft blue water. Every shaman has her own sacred spot, her point of entry into the spirit world, and this warm pool of water in the Arizona desert was the place where each of Carla's journeys began.

She dipped deep into the water, asking it to wash away her preconceptions and doubts, then climbed out onto the bed of smooth, warm stones around the edge of the pool. She turned eastward and called out in a soft whistle asking her familiar spirits to be close to her now. Then following the path of the sun, she repeated the incantation in all four directions. Once fully connected to the powerful beings who sit beside her, unseen but well known, she spoke her intention out loud, "Please help me learn why Timmy and Deb's lives have intersected with such purpose, and please bring Timmy and Deb any healing they may need." Turning toward the northeast, she caught hold of a knot on the tail end of a thick silk rope that hung down from the heavens.

Carla climbed skyward, up and up through the sun-drenched sky, up through the top layers of the atmosphere where the ozone collects in a sun-gilded mist, an air so thin yet so rich that each breath lasts a thousand years, until reaching the subtle membrane of smoke that divides the worlds. The rope itself pulled her through and she found herself surrounded by the chimerical dancing light of the Upper World.

Immediately to her left, a brick fountain drained into yet another pool of healing waters where Carla had washed many a sick animal — whoever said that cleanliness is next to Godliness didn't know how close to the mark they were. But today, Carla turned to her right and headed out across a broad, silvery plain, an area that seemed both vast and close, shimmering in and out like an oasis. This landscape might have appeared dizzying and featureless to some, but Carla read its subtle features like an experienced tracker, and she set off into it with calm assurance. Unlike our world, where some creatures remain aimless throughout their entire lives, in Non-Ordinary Reality you can't get anywhere at all unless you know where you're going. This is the reason a Shaman knows better than to ever make a journey without establishing a firm intention before setting off.

The landscape soon resolved itself into something resembling the English countryside on a summer's day: moist brown paths tamped gently into the land by generations of feet and hooves meandered through a rumpled patchwork quilt of fields, all patterned with neat rows of vegetable crops — a velvet patch of parsley here, the paisley heads of cabbages there, bright calicos of corn, tomatoes and carrots, all hemmed in by lacy ruffles of morning glory climbing over the tumbledown skeletons of runaway boxwood hedges.

At the far corner of a fallow field dotted with daisies and wild strawberries, Carla turned down a narrow lane alive with the gossipy chatter of wrens and starlings, and shaded by enormous, gently snoring elms. Careful not to wake them, she ambled toward a thatch-roofed cottage set in a sunny clearing. She stopped at a pergola set in a low wall made of river rock and unlatched a white wooden gate covered in bluebells and honeysuckle. Through the gate, a double row of hollyhocks, outlined a flagstone path. Off to the left, an herb garden flowered with lavender, thyme, marshmallow, chamomile and hyssop, and to the right, a wrought-iron café table and two slightly rusty ice-cream chairs occupied a small, circular patch of lawn at the center of a courtyard, beyond which lay the entrance to the cottage.

"Amber?" Carla called out, though the squeaky hinge on the cottage's screen door announced her arrival. "It's me, Carla!"

"In here," called a golden voice from somewhere near the back of the house. "You're just in time. I could use your help with these buttons."

Carla stepped through the threshold to the bedroom and saw her teacher, Amber, standing in front of a long, oval mirror. Amber's cloud of red hair rested on her bare shoulders. Her feet, too, were bare as usual, but in between she was swathed in a gown of pale gold moiré silk, ruffled at the neck and nipped in at the waist, with a voluminous bustle at the back and full, bell sleeves bedecked with gold, copper and flame-colored ribbons at the shoulders. She was just fastening a pair of long, white fingerless gloves to her wrists with dozens of tiny, seed-pearl buttons.

"Oh my goodness, what's the occasion?" Carla gasped.

Amber shot a bemused glance toward Carla's all-too-habitual denims and T-shirt, then squeezed her eyes shut and opened them wide and round before letting them settle into a soft cat-like gaze. Usually, Amber's eyes were a deep emerald green, a trait handed down from her Scottish ancestors, but from time to time, when she was feeling particularly feline, they flashed gold.

One of the things Amber had taught Carla long ago was that humans and animals were often aligned. Some people were cattish, while others were doggish, and still others were birdish or horseish, or some combination thereof. Amber's alliance was pure feline.

She smiled. "I know what you came for, dear, now get out of those hopeless clothes and put on something appropriate for the occasion. We're going to a party."

Amber and Carla had been friends for many years, and had seen and tasted dozens of adventures and drunk many hundreds of cups of Amber's home-grown chamomile tea together, and generally Amber was happy to accept Carla's fashion predilections, but not today.

"I've laid out several things. The blue would be smashing with your complexion, or the cinnamon brocade with the black and white ruffle, but if I know you, you'll want that one over there."

Carla was, in fact, drawn to the simple white gown Amber indicated. The dress had a subtle, iridescent sheen to it, and when she picked it up and held the soft fabric to her cheek it smelled exactly like kitten's breath. Amber grinned in recognition, wrinkling her nose and winking. "Who needs a dry cleaner's when you've got a litter of tabbies on the back porch to lick your laundry clean?"

Carla slipped into the ball gown, and Amber turned her around for inspection, "Now that's more like it!" she said, nodding in approval.

"Who is throwing the party?" Carla asked. "This dress is kinda heavy, you know."

"It's supposed to be heavy," Amber sighed, adding a crystal topped golden scepter to her outfit. "It lends you gravitas. I'm not sure who our host will be. But Timmy's the one who invited us."

At this bit of news, Carla forgot all about her clothing. "Well, in that case," she said, "let's hit the trail."

They left through the back door of the cottage, which opened onto a sheer bluff with a spectacular view of Space. At the edge of the bluff, they lifted their skirts and started down a blind stairway that curved and dipped precipitously. "Some of the steps appear to be missing," Amber whispered, "but they're not."

At the first such missing step, Carla tested the air with her right toes and failed to find a foothold. It wasn't until she transferred her weight completely to her right foot that the thin air decided to support her. You know, Carla thought to herself, Non-Ordinary Reality is as full of rewards for one's faith as the Middle World is of things that test it.

"I couldn't agree more," Amber said. "Oh, look, there are lights ahead."

The going leveled out until they found themselves on a clay path lit with strings of hanging lanterns. They followed it all the way up to a clearing in the darkness that opened before them suddenly, emerging straight into a sunny afternoon that sat in the middle of the darkness the way a bright green meadow might suddenly appear in the middle of a forest of gloomy trees. In the heart of the clearing was a colonnaded pavilion, alive with music and happy, singsong voices.

"Here we are," Amber said.

Strains of a string quartet, feminine laughter and the sound of tinkling glass filtered out across the lawn, growing louder as they approached.

A butler in black tie and a fur waistcoat greeted them at the top of the steps. "Good eve-a-ning, Ladies," he said, drawing each word out to include at least three syllables. "In-vi-ta-tions please."

Amber drew an envelope with gilded edges out from the sleeve of her dress and handed it to the butler, who genuflected in a complicated way, and turned to lead them in to the party.

"Is this what's called a tea dance?" Carla wondered.

"I don't know," Amber shrugged. "Not my era."

Inside the pavilion was one large ballroom, sparkling with crystal chandeliers, beneath which a sea of elegant, Victorian ladies swayed to and fro to the music, mewling and purring sweetly to each other and stroking the cats they each sported on their arms like giant, furry corsages.

Amber led the way, nodding and smiling and offering up admiring ooh!s and aah!s as the ladies held up their feline ornaments for Carla and Amber to admire.

"It's some kind of cat show," Amber whispered.

"I think I've read about this," Carla said. "But look! See how their outfits match their cats!"

It was true: A ruddy middle-aged woman with maroon hair and dressed in a purple silk caftan wore a pair of mauve

Manxes draped across her ample bosom like fox stoles. She was chatting with another grand dame in a pumpkin colored frock who absent-mindedly stroked the long, sleek body of an orange tabby that clung contentedly to her collar by its pearly claws. Beside them, a pretty young woman, probably the pumpkin's daughter, stared at the floor through lashes the color of daffodils while a fluffy white kitten with lemon yellow eyes lay curled in a basket that hung on her arm.

"At-ten-tion, lay-deez!" a man who could have been the twin of the butler cried, stepping into the middle of the ballroom and clapping his hands above his head to get their attention. "May I have your att-t-ten-sheeee-on!"

In their white gloves, the master of ceremony's fluttering hands looked like a pair of doves, and all the cats' eyes narrowed and snapped into focus. The ladies were somewhat less impressed and kept chattering on at each other.

Just then, a little girl appeared at the man's side and tugged hard on his coattail, as if she were ringing a bell. She held in her arms a gray cat that was almost as big as she was. The girl struggled to balance the languid cat's slippery, slinky weight, and he wasn't helping her any by twisting and turning limply in her arms as if he were nothing but so many pounds of liquid fur. The girl boosted him over her shoulder, then gave the man's coattail another pull, while the gray cat peered over her shoulder until his gaze met Carla's, and he distinctly winked.

"Amber, I think we have our Timmy!" Carla said, pointing.

The man bent down impatiently, and the girl whispered in his ear, then pointed surreptitiously at Carla and Amber. The man straightened, plucked the gray cat out of the girl's clutches, then marched straight over to them with an oily smile plastered beneath his curled and waxed moustache. He stopped, clicked his heels, and proffered the cat to Carla with another esoteric flourish. "I believe, Madame, that this eeez who you are looking for?"

Carla looked at Amber.

"Just go along with it," the cat said to her in a surprisingly deep voice. "Say, 'Thank you, Sir.'"

Carla accepted the cat and, not knowing quite what else to do, curtseyed. "Thank you, sir," she said.

Satisfied, the man gave a little bow, turned on his heel, and left.

Carla waved her thanks to the girl, who smiled and scampered off.

"She told the judge she found me in the bathroom," the cat said.

"Are you Timmy?" Carla asked.

"Yeah, I'm Timmy," he said, licking a paw.

"Ooooh, what a gorgeous creature, so pretty!" Carla glanced up and smiled at the pink chiffon woman who was offering her comments as she passed by, and Carla murmured a nice compliment about the lady's matching apricot kitty in return.

"Lord have mercy!" Carla said to Amber, smiling through clenched teeth. "Now what do we do?"

"Well, we came here to find out something important about Timmy and his family," Amber said. "What you have in your arms is a part of Timmy's soul that was lost. Now you can take it back to him. You've done good work here, Carla, you have what you came for. But if you're patient, there's more we can accomplish."

Amber gestured toward an imposing matron in a stiff,

42

gunmetal gray dress, a tower of hair the color and texture of steel wool atop her head. The woman held a gray cat with a white tip on its tail. Sensing their eyes on him, the cat turned and stared at Carla and Amber with a smug, disdainful air.

"You know what to do," Amber said.

Carla took the lead as they approached the gray lady and her arrogant cat, which spat something unintelligible to humans at Timmy as soon as they were within hissing distance. The woman smiled charmingly. "My dears, have you tried the petit fours? They're lovely!"

"Why no," said Carla. "Thank you, I shall."

"Don't eat anything!" Amber whispered urgently from behind.

"Yes, ma'am!" Carla whispered back.

"And watch your feet!" Amber said.

Carla looked down to see that the shiny marble floor was pocked with kitty refuse.

"This is not at all what it seems, this place," Amber said in a low voice. "We need to get that cat away from that woman. But here's the hitch; she needs to give it to us willingly."

"There's no way," Carla said.

"There is," said Amber. "Trust me." Carla felt the familiar sense of surrendering to Amber's farseeing wisdom. "We're going to give her Timmy in exchange. Don't worry, it will work."

"Got it," Carla said, and sidled up coyly to the gray lady. "Excuse me, ma'am," she said. "I was wondering, my mother has such a fondness for gray kitties, and she has admired yours so. She sees that your kitty is so striking with your dress, but you see, she lost a kitty like yours recently, and it hurts her

43

so..." Carla bit back a sob.

The woman's keen eyes narrowed. "You want my kitty, don't you?"

Carla straightened. "Yes, ma'am, I do, frankly."

"What will you give me in exchange?"

Carla glanced back at Amber, who nodded gravely and transmitted a tingling sensation into Carla's side. Recognizing the hint, Carla said, "I'll give you all the gold in my pocket, and I will give you my cat."

As if Carla had said the magic words, the woman turned toward her and stretched out both hands, pouring the gray cat into Carla's waiting arms, where it slipped into her body, taking refuge deep beneath her skin. "Oh!" Carla cried in surprise as she tried to assess the nature of the spiritual being nestled within her. "Oh my!" It felt distinctly like the spirit of a lost little girl. "Is that you, Debra?" Carla whispered.

"Shh!" Amber cautioned. "Now hand her Timmy."

Carla held out the big gray cat she still held in her arms, but saw as she did so that, in the confusion, Amber had used some sleight of hand to exchange the real Timmy for a stuffed one. "Let's go!" Amber hissed. Timmy peeked out from deep within the bell of her ruffled sleeve. "Before Old Ironsides figures out the switcheroo!"

"Pretty, pretty kitty!" the woman cooed as Amber and Carla scurried for the door and flew back the way they had come, emerging from darkness through dawn, back to Amber's safe and sacred gardens.

Amber gave a triumphant, rowdy whoop as they burst through the door of the cottage and Timmy leaped from hiding and danced around their legs in jubilation.

"Oh, that was a riot!" Amber howled, her cheeks hectic with color, tears of laughter winking at the corners of her eyes. She shrieked again, slapped both knees, and slumped against the doorjamb, bending nearly double.

"Why Amber," Carla said, the beginnings of an infectious chuckle building in her gut, "I haven't heard you laugh this hard since you told me all those jokes from your days as a farm girl. Oh, my!"

Amber stood upright and pushed herself off of the wall. "Let's get out of these clothes. I can hardly breathe in this get-up," she gasped.

"That's the second best plan you've had today" Carla said, relishing the genius of the switch, and transforming her trappings into the world's most comfortable garment, a well-worn, T-shirt emblazoned with an Icelandic horse.

"And now," Amber said, when she was back in her more usual flowing white shift, girded loosely with a jeweled belt, "Let's get these souls back where they belong."

Debra was sound asleep, with Timmy curled at the foot of her bed, when Carla and Amber crept noiselessly through her bedroom window. Amber carried Timmy's lost soul in her arms, and Debra's child-self still lay safe in Carla's heart chakra.

Carla bent over the bed and cupped her hands at the top of Debra's head, then gently blew her soul back into its rightful body. Amber did the same for Timmy, who purred and stretched contentedly, opening his eyes to gaze at them placidly, without the slightest show of alarm.

Carla stroked Debra's head. "In another lifetime, long ago," she explained quietly to the sleeping woman, "an unhappy woman stole you away. You were a child, and she stole you and turned you into a cat. Timmy was your guardian, but he got separated from you, and he couldn't protect you from the lonely lady, or get you back from her. So he waited patiently till you were ready and the circumstances were just right. It is good that you recognized him and that you asked for help! That way he could reunite you with the part of yourself that has been missing for so long. He will be your protector now, too."

"That's right," said Timmy. "And this time I'm not going to screw up!"

Carla smiled at him. "No, you're not, are you?"

"No!" Timmy said. "We're going to be fine. I'm going to rub her legs. But I have to tell you, when she leaves the house it bothers me a little bit. I try to go with her. My spirit tries to go with her. If she'd carry a picture of me it would help me a lot."

Carla nodded. "Tomorrow, when I talk to Debra in Ordinary Reality, I'll tell her to take a beautiful picture of you and put it in her purse. That will help you do your job."

"Yes," he said. "Yes, that would be splendid!"

"Debra is going to feel a solidness and completeness that she hasn't before," Carla said. "But she may also start experiencing memories, funny dreams, things from those many lives half-lived because of the lost soul. She'll experience those memories just as she would a novel about herself."

Timmy blinked and nodded sagely. "Tell her not to forget the photograph," he purred as he closed his eyes contentedly and stretched against the curve of Debra's sleeping form.

"Goodnight, Timmy," Amber said. "Sweet dreams," Carla added, as the two shamans stole silently over the windowsill and vanished back into the night.

46

This session helped Timmy heal from the traumas he carried and prepared him to fulfill his more urgent tasks. After this session he quickly settled into himself, and into the household. It wasn't long before he announced to Deb, "I want to go to a cat show!" "A What!?" she exclaimed. Deb had never even considered going to a cat show, much less participating in one. But Timmy wasn't to be denied. She asked me to investigate his reasons, and in a second journey, he told me that he needed to meet a white cat there who alone could impart some special cat lore he needed to know.

Being a cooperative sort, Deb groomed Timmy to perfection and went to the next cat show in Dallas. He was restless and uncooperative at first, but Deb reminded him the show was his idea. So he focused just long enough to win the initial judging. Then Deb moved his cage to the finalist's area, where he was placed next to a great, fluffy white cat. That was it! Timmy locked eyes with that cat and they remained intently focused on one another for the rest of the show. Deb had to ask him to break his reverie just long enough for the final judging – which he easily won. After accepting his prize, he immediately returned to his intense conversation with the white cat.

Deb and I are still not quite sure what the two cats were talking about. They can't explain it to us — frankly, it is over our heads. That's the amazing thing about these brilliant cats. We are just blessed to be in their presence.

– Carla

But I can't catch things because I don't have claws! Do you know how frustrating it is, not having claws?

Aria, Rebel Without a Claw

Do you have any idea what it takes to get a formally trained clinical psychologist to call a shamanic healer in to solve a behavior problem? In Ellen's case, the last straw came when she awoke one morning to a rushing sound accompanied by a sharp, acrid smell. She turned her head to find her Maine Coon cat, Aria, peeing on her pillow. Needless to say, she called me that very same day.

Amber was so stunned she almost burst out laughing. Carla, being the mistress of nine very mortal felines and one of *Nature's Miracle* Pet Odor Remover's very best customers, knew the situation wasn't so humorous.

"Right on her pillow?" Amber repeated yet again. "While she was actually sleeping on it?"

"Yes, Amber," Carla said for the umpteenth time. "Right under the poor woman's nose."

Once Amber's shock had subsided, she set about preparing for the trip to Ellen and Aria's malodorous abode. "I can't wait to meet her," Amber bubbled. "The cat, I mean. Though I'm sure Ellen is a very nice lady. But just wait until I get my paws on that bold little scamp!"

"Hands, you mean," Carla corrected.

Amber shrugged. "Hands, paws, whatever. Here's what I was looking for!" She took a translucent glass flacon down from one of her crowded shelves.

Carla raised an eyebrow. "You're going to cover up the stink with perfume?" she said.

"No, no," Amber said. "This isn't perfume. It's more like a genie in a bottle, only much better. And since we're on that theme, let's take the magic carpet today."

So Carla and Amber rode the magic carpet down to the Middle World , skimming over rows and rows of orderly suburban rooftops until they came to a house that lay at the far end of a cul de sac in an older neighborhood, a street that butted right up against an undeveloped riparian wilderness alive with crickets and toads, snakes and salamanders.

"I recognize this place," Amber said. "This riverbed is like a Motel 6 for migrating herons and whooping cranes. It's cat heaven, too, that's for sure! If Aria's unhappy living here, then there must be something terribly wrong."

"We're about to find out," Carla said as the carpet swept them in through an open window and deposited them right in the middle of the living room floor.

Aria was sitting in an armchair, licking her meaty paws. She was a silvery-gray cat with a wide, elegant face, intelligent eyes and a haughty, disdainful bearing, even as she reclined in the lap of suburban luxury. She reminded Carla of some of her more precocious students at the college, the ones who had yet to learn that they didn't know everything, or that being young and gorgeous was not, in fact, a talent.

50

"Hello, Aria," Carla said. "My name is Carla."

Aria looked up at her and did that blinking thing that cats do. "Yes?" she said, then continued licking her paw.

Carla decided that a professorial tone was indeed in order. "Aria," she said firmly. "This morning your mother was rudely awakened by the smell of fresh cat pee in her face."

Aria looked up at Carla with a startled expression.

Carla continued. "So she asked me to come, because she's a bit at a loss as to what to do. She doesn't appreciate it when you pee on her pillow."

"I know," Aria said smugly, flicking an ear. "That's why I did it."

"I expected as much," Carla said casually, not wanting to give Aria the satisfaction of shocking her. "Actually, I'm just here to understand why. This is my friend Amber."

Amber held the glass bottle out in front of Aria's nose. "And this is my little friend," Amber said in a singsong voice.

Aria's whiskers shot up, and she stretched her neck out, sniffing anxiously toward the bottle. She rose into a crouch, then swatted at it. "Gimme!" she whined. "Gimme that! Gimme that!"

Amber teased her, waving the bottle just beyond her reach. Aria followed it with her eyes, as intensely focused on the object as if it were a vial of catnip. Satisfied by the strength of Aria's reaction, Amber gave in and let her have the object.

Aria grasped the bottle between her paws and teeth and pulled it close to her chest.

"What exactly is in there?" Carla asked.

"You'll see," Amber promised. She turned to Aria. "Aria!" she said sharply, to get the cat's attention, then changed her tone to one of gentle invitation. "Would you like to take a walk down by the creek?"

Without a moment's hesitation, Aria let go of the bottle, hopped down from her chair and led the way out through a sliding glass door in the dining room, through a hole in the fence, and out into a field that stretched all the way to a small, rocky creek bed. Amber picked up the bottle and followed.

Now, that's very interesting, Carla thought. Usually she and Amber carried a cat wherever they went, but Aria was very independent that way.

The creek was a typical California feeder creek, a thick slick of water running over jagged rocks, surrounded by mud and grasses. "This is my creek!" Aria announced, stepping onto a high rock and surveying her own personal spread.

"What is it you like to do when you're here?" Amber asked.

"Well, I look for bugs along the shore, and I watch the water, but there are snakes, too, along the shore, that are fun to try to catch." Aria's proud posture slumped momentarily, and the cocky arrogance in her tone faded to bitterness. "But I can't catch them because I don't have claws! Do you know how frustrating that is, not having claws?"

"I can imagine," Amber said sympathetically, sitting down next to her and handing Aria the bottle once again. "Tell me what it's like not having claws."

"It's like a tree not having leaves," Aria said, "That's what it's like! It's like the sun not having rays. A cloud that never rains. Thunder with no lightning. Food with no water." Anger and sorrow choked off her voice.

Carla sat down in the grass next to Amber and Aria. "So are you angry that you don't have claws?" she ventured. "And does that have something to do with why you pee all over the

52

house?"

"I don't pee all over the house!" Aria snapped.

"You pee in the parts of the house where you know your mother doesn't want you to."

"I don't know," Aria said crossly, feeling a deep growl forming in her chest. "I just get angry. I just feel angry. I feel this sense of indignation come over me, like my life was put upon me and there's nothing I can do about it, and I'm stuck..." She glowered and turned her rage to the bottle, rolling over and attacking it with the good claws on her rear feet.

"Aria," Amber said quietly. "Could I have the bottle back, just for a moment?'

Aria rolled off the bottle, and Amber held it aloft in the sunlight. Its contents had turned a livid green, the color of battery acid. "Hmm," Amber said. "That's good. We're almost there." She put the bottle back down in front of the cat, but Aria appeared to have lost interest in it.

"I'm not sure that belongs to me," she said, pushing it away from her with a paw.

Amber smiled at Carla. "And that, my dear, is how we put the genie back in the bottle!"

"Ohhhh," Carla grinned. "We're doing a new kind of extraction."

"Exactly," said Amber. "Extraction of emotion. Soon we will find out what the root cause of it is, but the first thing we had to evoke a memory that brought up the emotion and have the anger itself go into the bottle, where it won't be as destructive for her behavior. That's why the bottle is now green, green with anger."

Amber picked up the bottle and wrapped it up carefully in a golden cloth, then stood. "Aria," she said. "If you'll wait right here, Carla and I will be back in a few minutes."

"Whatever," Aria said with an attempt at feigned indifference, though she couldn't keep the relief and gratitude she felt from creeping in.

Amber and Carla flew quickly over the trees and mountaintops, flying fast and far, until they were soaring over the open ocean, where Amber let go of the green bottle. She and Carla lingered to watch it sink under the crashing waves. "By the time this bottle washes ashore, it will be transformed into something beautiful, and the genie will be granting wishes, not pain," Amber declared. "Cool huh?"

"Yeah," Carla said. "Way cool."

"Well," said Amber. "We'd better get back to Aria. There's still a whole lot of healing to be done."

So they returned to the creek bed, where Aria tried her best to look unfazed. "I was thinking," she said with feigned casualness. "Is there any way I can maybe get my claws back?"

"Wow," Carla cried. "What a great idea! Yes, Aria, you can get your claws back, and we can help you do it. I don't know if they'll pop out of your feet, but by the time we leave you, the spirit of your claws will be back in your paws, that I can promise you."

Aria grinned. "Well, what are we waiting for?"

Amber whistled, and the magic carpet appeared. "May I?" she asked Aria, and the big cat butted her outstretched hand in assent. So Amber picked up Aria and settled her onto the carpet between herself and Carla, then she pulled out her well-worn map of the Upper World. "We are looking for the home of the Maine Coon tribe," she said, more to the map

54

than to her passengers. "Ah, there it is, thank you!"

And off they went, climbing high through the many worlds that lay between Aria's earthly home and her ancestors' heavenly abode, a place where the ground was covered with a layer of fallen pine needles as thick as a mattress, and the air was fragrant with the smell of resin and pine oil.

"It's beautiful," Carla cried. "What are these trees? Are they Pines, Cedars, Douglas Fir?"

"We're Pines!" the trees whispered, tickling her under the chin with their long green needles. "White Pines!"

"Yes of course," Carla said. "I'm sorry, I've never been to Maine."

The carpet settled on the springy mat of needles. "This place looks familiar," Aria said, just as a fine, fat Maine Coon tomcat came sashaying out from behind a granite boulder.

"As it should," he admonished her, then turned his attention to Amber and Carla. "Welcome. Who are you?"

"I am Carla, and this is Amber," Carla said, bowing. "And this is Aria."

"So you are. Fol-low!" the big cat commanded, and turned with a magisterial swish of his great bushy tail.

They followed, mesmerized by the thump whump, thump whump of the big cat's tail, so rich and powerful it seemed to be swinging his haunches back and forth, rather than the other way around.

They walked into a clearing where more big, gray, brush-tailed cats came, all of them Maine Coons. Their guide pointed them toward an older cat with a brownish coat and strong eyebrow markings. "This one will answer your questions."

Carla looked at Amber, and Amber stepped back a step and for a moment abdicated her role. "Well, what do you want to ask them, Carla?"

Taking a quick breath, Carla gathered her courage. Then she turned to face the brown cat with the heavy brow.

"Oh Great Maine Coons," she began. "We have come to you today on behalf of Aria. She feels great anger in her body and behaves in her household in a way that is very disruptive to her person."

The cats looked at each other and whispered their reactions in titterings and tisks.

Carla took a breath. "Aria pees in the house, and poops in the house. And what's more, she does it with anger in her heart. She tells us that she is angry, and overwhelmingly so. We have removed the intrusive residue of anger from her, oh Great Ones, but we have come to ask you why she is so angry. We have come to ask for the story of anger as you Maine Coons know it."

The big leader rose, fluffed his tail, then sat again, this time with it curled to his left. "Is that all?"

"No, oh Great One. We have come to ask you if your tribe could restore to Aria the spirit of her claws."

"Right," he said curtly. "Let's do that first."

Carla and Amber stood back as the cats led Aria to the center of the clearing and gestured for her to sit. Then all of the cats began to walk around and around her, falling into concentric circles. An inner circle walked counter-clockwise, while an exterior circle walked clockwise, and another circle walked counter-clockwise again, and so on, to the edge of the clearing. Together, they began to mew and purr, mew and purr, their voices mingling to form a complicated, percussive

56

rhythm, a music unlike anything Carla had ever heard.

"Aria!" the brown cat commanded. "Hold out your right front paw!"

Aria extended her paw. The cats began to circle tighter and faster, until the electricity crackled and sparked off of their shimmering coats in the crisp northern air and SMACK! ZAP! A blue flash erupted like lightning, and five sharp, shiny claws sprang from Aria's right front paw.

"Now the left!" the brown cat ordered. The cats switched direction, and the process was repeated. Again, the power of the cats built until there came another clap of thunder and lightning. Aria gasped in pleasure and awe as she felt the power of the claw return to her left foot. She stretched each paw out in front of her, extending the claws and looking at their sharp white points.

Then content, she sat down in that way cats do when they crouch and tuck their feet in front of them, and purred.

The cats disbanded their circle and proceeded to settle into familial groups around the clearing, purring and grooming one another, taking special care to clean each millimeter of each others ears, and sharing special memories of their past and future lives on worlds across the galaxies. A young cat stepped forward.

"You have asked for the story of why we are angry; I will tell you!" he shouted in a voice as broad and loud as a television evangelist. "May the telling of this help the brothers and sisters who are stuck in the vortex of anger!"

The other cats settled into stillness, listening, and he began: "One day in the forest, the lightning struck the tree and the tree broke in half! It split. It did not catch fire, but it remained wounded. Woodpeckers came in and pecked at the

57

interior pulp. The tree felt violated and could do nothing.

"At the same time that happened, a man chopped off the head of a chicken and the body ran around, as they do.

"And at the same time that happened a man caught a fish and ripped it up out of the water... and gutted it.

"And at the same time that happened, a lion caught a calf, and the mother elk screamed... She screamed.

"And of all these creatures, it was the lion who said, 'Oh what have I done? What have I done?' And as she munched down the calf, she said 'Is there any way to do this without causing so much pain?' And she answered herself, 'I don't know. But it's easier to contemplate these things on a full stomach.'

"That lioness, the hunter, the mother of all cats, walked away from the carcass with a full stomach and a heavy heart. The crows came in and ate the remains, and the mother elk went into mourning, and the next year, she mated again."

And with that, the young orator cat stood down, and the other cats in the clearing began to purr their applause—an earnest murmur that rose to a muted crescendo, then slowly died.

Carla waited until the only sound left in the clearing was twitter of a lark and the distant drone of a woodpecker.

"So, Great Cats," she ventured hesitantly. "How does this explain Aria's anger?"

All of the cats turned to her. Their eyes widened, and some of them shook their heads as if they couldn't believe what they were seeing or hearing.

Carla felt like an idiot, but there was no hope for it, so she just smiled, heaved a big sigh and shrugged apologetically.

58

"Well at least you get that you don't get it!" The old brown cat said.

"Yes sir," Carla said. "You'd be right about that."

"Imagine how frustrating it is when they think they get it and they don't!" the young storyteller said. "Do you realize how many people think they get it and they don't???!"

"Well yes, actually," Carla replied. "I do have some sense of that."

The cats seemed prepared to let the whole thing go at that, but Carla decided to make one more attempt. "Kitties," she said. "Forgive my denseness. But I need more from you. Could you give me more? How often does someone come and beg to learn, beg you to teach them?"

The cats murmured among themselves. Carla heard rueful laughter here and there.

"Ah, yes," said the brown cat. "Never, come to think of it. 'Never' would be the answer to that question."

Just then a huge, flea-bitten, rag-eared old cat with a palsied quiver to his walk that only magnified his air of authority broke through the ranks and marched up to stand before Carla. "Never... come... to... think... of... it!" he declared in a booming voice.

The ancient cat then settled onto his rickety haunches and grinned at Carla and — oh my goodness — he hadn't a single tooth in his battered old head. If you've never seen a cat with a toothless grin, know that it is quite a fearsome sight.

And then he spoke again, his voice as lush and robust as his body was feeble. "It is the anger of youth," he said. "The anger of contradictions. The anger of frustration at circumstances they cannot change. In this cat's case, the cat is a hunter, and she wants to be outside at night, it is *that* simple. And the cat had residual anger from her claws being ripped out of her paws — *and who can blame her?!*"

The cats in the clearing meyowled in indignation. Carla heard them muttering to each other in earnest tones:

"I got my claws. You got your claws?"

"Yep, I got my claws. You got yours?"

"Yeah, I got mine, how about you?

"Oh, we've got our claws, absolutely!"

"Well, guess what!" The elder cat bellowed angrily. "I don't have teeth!" He grinned bitterly. "But I've got my claws!"

The cats in the clearing hissed and yowled and raked the air with their claws with relish.

"Carla," the wise old cat continued gently. "You need to know that only the very youngest of us go to Earth, and so many of the Maine Coon cats on earth are really just young, young, young ones of our tribe. And like your angry youth, trapped in a world they struggle against, ours are trapped in a world that they struggle against, and they've not developed the emotional maturity or the philosophical contemplation to manage their emotions. And this, my dear, is why the Maine Coons sometimes behave in manners disruptive to their households."

"We send them to boarding school!" A heckler among the crowd cried out. "Heh! Heh! Heh!"

"I see," said Carla. "So you're helping your kitties get their education by putting them with families on Earth, eh?"

"That's one way of putting it," he answered. "It's part of their process, indeed, to spend time on Earth."

With this, he rose and blew into Aria's ears, one after the

other, then offered her a final benediction: "May you be graced with the capacity to understand that the reason you are in the house so much is to save your fanny from those things that would rip you asunder," he said to her. "And may you be blessed with the knowledge that your woman Ellen works with you in the way she does with pure love."

He looked back at Carla and his eyes glowed as he said, "Sometimes we need our people to teach us what pure love is. Just as people youth needs to learn, so cat youth needs to learn. You thank your Ellen for doing a very good job!"

He turned to go, then paused. "Tell her, if you would, that I recommend that she construct an outdoor run for this cat, somewhere safe where she can go to feel the spirit of the night." And he stalked away without another backward glance. One by one, the rest of the Maine Coon tribe filed out of the clearing after him.

Carla felt something warm push against her leg and looked down to see Aria nuzzling her, stretching and preening, jockeying coyly for affection the way that well-loved, happy cats will do.

"I will tell her," Carla promised, stroking the top of Aria's head. "I will tell her." She looked to Amber, who nodded ever so gently, so as not to let the tears in her eyes spill over.

Ellen reported that Aria was really much better immediately following the session, and for many weeks she was much more conscientious about not using the house for a litter box. Ellen also decided to give Aria the freedom to go outside, which Aria very much appreciated. The behavior change, though, was not

complete. After a period, Aria resumed peeing on things, mostly to make statements and to get Ellen's attention. Ellen says this is particularly the case when she makes choices for Aria, such as whether to be inside or out. Ellen also notes that Aria still misses her claws, as she tries to scratch wood frequently, to no avail.

Getting a cat to stop making urinary statements is the hardest thing I try to accomplish. It is harder than curing "terminal" illnesses, harder than getting a vicious dog to become sweet, harder than anything I have faced as a shamanic communicator. I have indeed been successful, but often, the session's main value is in helping the guardian understand their kitty and manage the situation. But I keep trying, with the understanding, of course, that the outcomes are mixed. Cats! Some of them really do have their own agendas.

That being said, this story is filled with magical images that frequently come up in shamanic healings involving an animal's spirit tribe: the circle of cats moving clockwise and counter clockwise at once, the return of lost spirit fragments to restore the wholeness of the soul, and the amazing knowledge that cats don't necessarily incarnate only on earth, but share their transcendent power and wisdom with other lands far beyond our reach.

— Carla

Would you like us to help you, Bum?

Bum in Love

The first weeks of winter are a time of utmost clarity. The icy wind sweeps all doubt and ambivalence before it, leaving behind a world that is crisp and clean. But be careful, because the edges of this world are razor-sharp and its perfect vistas are oh, so very brittle!

This is a story straight out of the cold, cruel world, about a stray cat named Bum who practically dares his owner to love him. Fortunately, no place on earth, or in the heavens above or below it, is so cold that it can't be reached by the warming effects of forgiveness, courage and compassion.

Ice sparkled on the hanging branches of the tree of life, and the air between its frozen leaves shimmered like the wake of a bright, elusive memory as Carla made her way through the woods toward Amber's cottage. As she drew near her destination, Carla heard a warm, golden voice singing a folksy song. Stepping off the path and into a frozen glen, she found Amber standing in the center of a sparkling amphitheater, her head and shoulders draped in a pale knitted cloak made of yarn spun from the white snow leopard's winter coat. Her pale, rounded arms conducted the shivering, tinkling song of a thousand icicles as they rubbed together like so many crystal bells — a pure sound that contrasted nicely with Amber's earthy lyrics, learned from the hands on her farm so many years ago.

The last chorus was a doozy, and when Amber finished and turned, taking Carla's chilly hands in hers, her cheeks were hectic with the mortal pleasure of song. "What was that tune?" Carla asked as Amber led the way back to her cottage.

Amber winked. "When you're as old as I am, I'll teach it to you."

Carla shook her head. Amber appeared to be a healthy woman enjoying the prime of her mid-thirties, but Carla knew that she had lived to be eighty-four years old on earth, and that her tenancy in the cozy, thatch-roofed cottage they now entered was practically limitless.

The interior of the cottage was warm and welcoming. The glow emanating from the fireplace overpowered the hard blue light that cut through the windowpanes, smelting it into a buttery gold liquid that was at once fresh and nourishing.

Carla settled into a deep leather armchair chair and drew a tartan lap rug over her knees. "I've come to see about a fellow named Bum," she said. "He's a big, scraggly black cat who arrived on Debra's doorstep a few months ago. He has a persistent heartworm problem and he's also suffering from a lingering case of coon hound paralysis."

"Bum," Amber said, the name pleasing her ear. She found a tune and sang "Bum-bum-bum, bum-bum, bum-bum-bum," as she ran her fingers over the heavy, leather-bound volumes on her bookshelf, then plucked out a green one with cryptic gold lettering down its spine.

Amber settled on the arm of Carla's chair, nipping a pair

66

of reading glasses onto the bridge of her nose and leafing through the book's sweet-smelling pages. "Aha, here we go," she said, holding out the book. Its pages were covered in text, but the words seemed to tremble and blur as Carla looked at them.

Amber laughed. "Don't work at it so hard," she said. "When you read a book here, all you need to do is open it and let the essence escape. Here, I'll show you!" Amber pulled the book away from Carla and bent over it, breathing deeply like a person intent on catching the aroma from a pot of fragrant soup abubble on a stove. Her eyes fell half-closed and she smiled, then snapped the book shut and rose to replace it on its shelf.

"Well?" asked Carla.

"My dear Carla," Amber said, "Would you please look in the kitchen, on the top shelf to the right of the stove? There's a pink cloisonné bottle with a brass stopper — yes, yes, that's the one."

Amber took the bottle from Carla, held it at arm's length, and unstopped it briefly, releasing a strong odor of camphor and pine oil. "That's the ticket," she said. "Whew! Let's get this show on the road! According to the *Book of Worms*, we mustn't delay."

Together, Amber and Carla stepped out into the shimmering day, and before they had taken three steps down the garden path — whoosh! They found themselves flying upward, darting through the spreading branches of the tree of life, up, up, up to the land of cats. They landed in the yard of a farmhouse where hundreds of white cats milled lazily about. Posh creatures with dense, voluptuous coats the color of newly fallen snow, they rubbed against each other and mewled expectantly.

"This doesn't look like anywhere we're likely to find Bum," Carla said skeptically. "He's a black kitty, and from what I understand, he's a little rough around the edges. And if I'm not mistaken, he's still on earth — I mean in the Middle World."

"We just need to pick up some supplies," Amber said, "Then we'll be off."

The ground was so thick with cats that Carla and Amber had to clutch each other by the elbows to be sure neither one of them stepped on a tail or a paw as they picked their way gingerly toward the farmhouse's front door.

Suddenly the door opened inward, and a gnarled old farmer fought his way out through the tide of incoming cats. "Shoo! Shoo!" he cried, waving his arms and swinging his feet to clear a path. "This way, Miss Amber. Don't mind the bleedin' rascals, you can't hurt 'em!" He beckoned them enter.

Carla and Amber stepped through the doorway into a small, dark room. The farmer knelt in front of a cedar chest, rummaging through its contents and cursing under his breath. "Blasted furballs!" he muttered. "What I wouldn't do for a big old coon hound right about now."

"It's a long story, but just think of this as a cross between penance and therapy," Amber whispered slyly to Carla behind her hand. "And from Mr. Oakley's attitude, I'd say he's still got a century or two of feline husbandry in his future."

"Aye, there's the one!" the farmer cried. He presented Amber with a fluffy white blanket. Amber stroked its pristine surface and smiled kindly at the old man. "It's lovely, Mr. Oakley. Thank you very much."

A flicker of a smile passed over his face before he noticed

with a start and a scowl that every single one of the white cats had crept in through the open door while he was distracted. Now their languid forms covered every inch of chair, bed, table and floor space in the tiny farmhouse. "Dag blast it!" Mr. Oakley cried, in a voice that contained more despair than anger.

"Believe it or not, that was progress!" Amber whispered with amusement as she led Carla back outside. "There's one more thing we need, and then we'll go find Bum." She stopped in front of a gnarled oak tree in the center of the farmyard, and gestured toward a hole in its trunk. "After you."

Sighing, Carla closed her eyes and leaped into the hole in the tree. Spinning like a drill bit, she burrowed deep into the tree, down through its roots and into the ground, where she eventually bumped right up against the hard, lacquered shell of a big black beetle.

"Ooof!" he said, giving her a good pinch on the arm as he pushed her away. "Careful there!"

"Sorry," Carla said, wincing. "I didn't see you."

"That's because I'm underground," the beetle snapped, waving his antennae like angry fists. "You're not supposed to see me! It's the middle of winter, for crying out loud! Hey, watch the larvae! Step on them again and I'll pinch you but hard!"

Just then, Amber tumbled out of Carla's tunnel.

"Oh," the beetle said grudgingly. "It's you."

Amber smiled sweetly. "Nice to see you, too, friend. Say, the larvae are looking mighty plump for so early in the season. You must be very pleased."

"We'll see," he clicked grudgingly.

"Are all beetles this grumpy?" Carla asked, still smarting from the pinch.

"As a species, they tend to be very dry," Amber said. "They make excellent public school principals."

"I'll say."

Amber held out her hand. The beetle poked its pincer into a patch of dirt still slick from larval digestive juices, and transferred a wet, sticky clump of it into Amber's cupped palm.

"Thank you very much," Amber said formally, secreting the handful of soil into a hidden pocket of her cloak. She smiled at Carla and led the way back up the tunnel and into the daylight.

"Now," Amber said, dusting off her white gown and adjusting the golden clasp of her cloak. "We are ready for our Mister Bum."

"Good," groused Carla, "I've had about all of the pinching and cursing I can take for one day."

Amber chuckled. "You shouldn't say things like that around here," she cautioned. "Oh, no, honey, I'm just teasing you," she said when she saw Carla's stricken face. "You're a hundred thousand lifetimes removed from any of the things you just saw. Don't worry about it."

"Thank goodness for that."

"Shall we take the express again?" Amber asked, taking Carla's hand and leaping into motion without further ado.

This time, they came to rest squarely in the Middle World, in a comfortable, if somewhat disorderly, parlor with a low, beamed ceiling and a picture window overlooking the seashore. Bum was there, rubbing up against the leg of a shabby overstuffed sofa.

Amber knelt and stroked Bum's back. His tail shot up and he put out his paws for more loving. She scooped him up into her arms and settled cross-legged onto the carpet, holding him close.

Here was a cat whose lifetime of misadventures had left him very much the worse for wear. Bum's eyes were cloudy with cataracts, his ears were notched and shredded, and his chapped nose was crosshatched with ancient claw marks. The pads of his clawless paws were cracked, sore and callused. His thin black fur had lost its gloss, and stood in thin patches as brittle as burnt grass. Carla shuddered to imagine the sorry state of Bum's tiny, pink heart after a lifetime of so much abuse.

Amber cradled him like a baby and wiped the crust from his eyes with a corner of her robe.

"First the tincture," she said. Carla removed the brass stopper from the pink bottle and handed it to Amber. She dabbed a drop of it on the tip of his scarred nose. He licked it off. She dabbed another drop at the base of his tail, and another on the top of his head. Then she rolled him over and parted the fur at his solar plexus, and placed a last drop right there.

"I can feel it!" Bum croaked in a spent, raspy voice.

"I'll bet you can!" Amber said, unfurling the white, fuzzy blanket from the Persian cat farm. At the sight of the blanket, Bum came alive. He pounced into it, pushing and burrowing with his head like a kitten. Amber smiled. "That's good," she said, then wrapped the playful, squirming Bum in the blanket and pulled it close to her chest. His head popped out from the top and he looked at Carla, then at Amber, and broke into a huge, rolling purr.

"Would you like us to help you, Bum?" Amber asked.

"Oh, yes!" Bum purred.

Amber produced the handful of dirt from the beetle's lair from the folds of her cloak, then dipped in a finger and rubbed it onto Bum's gums.

He smacked his lips. "That tastes like dirt!" he said.

"Yes, it does, Bum," Amber said kindly but firmly, "Now swallow it down."

Obediently, Bum swallowed hard.

"That will help cleanse out the heartworms," Amber informed Carla. Next, she examined Bum's clawless front paws. She placed one on each of her shoulders, then pressed him close to her chest, hugging him hard until he disappeared right inside of her body.

Smiling, Amber fidgeted — or, rather, Bum fidgeted, as he settled into a comfortable place inside her. Then Amber began to sing, and down from the sky fell threads of golden light, passing right through the heavy wooden roof of the house and falling in whorls on Amber's upturned face.

"There is something inside you that needs help?" the light whispered.

"Oh, yes," Amber sang. "Please encase it and heal it with your light."

Then the golden light turned to a fine, sparkling powder as it fell about Amber's head and shoulders and filled her lap. Amber happily sang as she rubbed and scrubbed, working the powder into every inch of her skin.

"Carla," Amber whispered. "Would you please see what is outside?"

72

Carla left the house and walked down to the shore, where she found nothing but a log rolling at the edge of the surf. She bent and tried to lift it, but the log was incredibly heavy and she couldn't seem to budge it an inch.

"May I help you with that?" boomed a man's voice from somewhere above her.

Carla whirled and saw a tall, bearded woodsman smiling down at her, a shiny axe stuck through his leather belt. "Y-yes, please," she said. The woodsman bent and hefted the log. It was heavy, even for him, but he wrestled it up from the surf and rested it on his broad shoulder. Carla held the door of the beach house open for him, though the woodsman was so tall he had to stoop just to step through the doorway and could not stand up to his full height once inside.

He laid the log on the rug in front of Amber, where she sat cross-legged and still, then bowed as best he could from his already crouched position. Amber nodded her thanks. "Would you be so kind as to split it open?" she asked.

The woodsman drew his axe and split the log open with a single, loud *whack!*

Out from the log spilled a company of spirits, shadowy and pale as the blue flames from a gas stove. They whirled and danced, whispering and moaning, cat-like in their motion. Carla found them difficult to look at, and she couldn't tell if this was because they were extremely dark or exceedingly bright. She only knew that of all the medicine Amber had summoned for Bum, these spirits were the most potent by far, and that Amber had taken Bum's soul into her own body in order to protect him from the full force of their power.

Amber unfolded her robes and Bum's scrawny black tail popped right out of her belly button. The shadowy blue-black cloud of spirits swarmed toward the tail, and licked it all over, the way cats do when they clean their young. "There, there, that's enough dears," Amber said, closing her robe again. She shooed the spirits gently back toward the log. On their way, they swirled close to Carla, pausing curiously and licking the back of her hand with their dusky tongues. She shivered at their touch, an ice-hot mixture of pain and pleasure that left her with a sensation she could only think of as *blooming*.

One by one, the spirits slipped back into the split grain of the log, which the woodsman again shouldered and returned to the surf. "Goodbye," Carla called, "Thank you."

Amber reached under her robe and pulled Bum out. He was damp, and shook himself, then stood swaying as he separated fully into his own being. As his coat dried, Carla could see that it already looked healthier than before. He looked at her for the first time. "Hello," he said amiably.

"Hello, Bum," Carla said. "I'm a friend of Deb's."

Bum settled down on the carpet and began grooming his much-improved self. "Are you?" he said. "It's very nice of you to come."

"The question I have is why have you come?" Carla said. "To Deb's house, I mean."

Bum smiled. "I came to help her find something," he said. "Something she lost."

"What do you mean?" asked Carla. "What did she lose?"

"Her compassion," Bum answered. "Deb had lost her belief in her own compassion." He chuckled. "But take one look at me! I'm such a mess, how could she not be compassionate toward me?"

Amber laughed. "Why Bum, you're proud of being a mess,

aren't you?"

Bum ducked his head. "Well, yes and no," he said. "It's my job, you see. But on the other hand, I'm really getting tired of it."

"In that case, Bum," Carla said, taking his two skinny paws in her hands, "are you willing to go on and finish dealing with this heartworm disease?"

Bum looked at Amber. "Do you really think you can get the little critters out of there?"

Amber shrugged. "All we can do is try." She laid the white blanket out on the floor. "Carla, you go get that salt shaker from the dining table, then stand on one corner of the blanket, over there. I'll stand here opposite you. Now, sprinkle the salt all over the blanket — that's right."

When the beautiful white blanket was fairly heaped with salt crystals, Amber held Bum up over it and shook him gently up and down. "Did you ever keep a garden, Carla?" Amber asked.

"My mother did," Carla said. "Why do you ask?"

"Because this is an old horticulturist's technique for dealing with garden slugs," she said. "It's just that it's a bit, er — well, Gothic."

"What does that mean?" Carla asked dubiously.

"You'll see," Amber said in a voice that was ominously grim, still shaking Bum steadily up and down over the blanket. Now the heartworms began to fall out of Bum's body, raining down on the white blanket like grains of overcooked rice. When their mucous-sheathed bodies hit the blanket they writhed and shrank, squirming wretchedly and making a caustic hissing sound. Amber shook Bum some more, and more worms tumbled down, landing on the blanket, and dissolving. Amber shook and shook him, until fewer and fewer worm spirits were left, and then she kept shaking him until there were none at all. The worms on the blanket had dissolved completely into a pile of pale, sticky goo.

Satisfied, Amber handed the slightly dizzy Bum over to Carla, then took what looked like a Hefty bag made of gold out of one of her many hidden pockets. Folding the blanket in on itself by gingerly plucking up the dry corners, she stuffed the entire gelatinous mess into it, giving the top a firm twist to seal it. "There! Follow me," she sang out happily as she skipped outside. Carla, still fighting down a sick feeling in the pit of her stomach, stumbled after her.

Amber hiked up her dress and waded out ankle-deep into the surf, holding the golden garbage bag out at arm's length. The ocean heaved up a great wave that tore the bag out of Amber's grasp and sucked it down, down, down and out, out, out, carrying its foul contents far out to sea. Only then did Carla manage to swallow the bile in her mouth. "Whew," she said. "I'm glad that's over. But it's going to be a while before I go swimming."

"We give these things to the ocean" Amber explained, "in order that they be transformed back into goodness." She shot Carla a wicked, playful grin. "You think that gob of dead worms was bad? Goodness knows where that log had been! Or rather, what it used to be! Come on, I'll race you back!" And she took off, running barefoot through the sand.

Back in the cabin, Amber scratched the top of Bum's head. "There, there, kitty," she cooed. "That's better, isn't it?"

"Muucch better," Bum purred. "Now if it weren't for this toothache, I'd feel like a kitten again."

76

"I brought some goldenseal and myrrh for that," Amber said.

"Is that why you were so mean when you first came to Deb's?" Carla asked. "Because your tooth ached?"

Carla felt a jolt in her heart as the image in Bum's mind flashed across to her: a white cat, angry and hissing, ears flat back, blood on its lips...

"Oh, Bum!" Carla exclaimed.

"She was my best friend," Bum said woefully, shrinking from Amber's caress now as if he didn't feel he deserved it, "and she abandoned me. Over an empty can of tuna fish. I doubt there's anything in your medicine bag that can cure a broken heart."

"Well," Carla said thoughtfully. "I wouldn't be so sure about that." She glanced at Amber inquiringly.

Amber nodded. "Go for it," she said.

Bum watched Carla with a curious, yet wary, expression as she went to the open doorway and stretched out her arms to the sky, giving a piercing whistle. A distant, powerful cry echoed in return, and Carla turned to face Bum. "I've just summoned my power animal, the one that helps me with soul retrievals. I'm going to journey to find the parts of your soul that are lost, so that I may restore them to you."

Carla gathered Bum into her arms, then kissed the top of his patchwork head and handed him back to Amber as the shadow of a giant osprey darkened the sky, bearing down amidst a thundering of wings.

The great bird never even touched the ground. Carla threw her arms around its slim, powerful neck as it swooped down, and together they took off into the sky, traveling so far and fast that days and nights flashed by like light falling through a stand of trees as you race by them on a speeding train. Soon, the bird settled down on the ground at a place where the moon shone on the flat white surface of a frozen lake.

"Look there," whispered the spirit of the lake. An eddy of snow pointed them toward a house, where a war was going on — a long war between two people. Angry voices echoed through the night; the sound of breaking crockery, then shrieks of pain, and a single sob. The back door opened and a man staggered out, cursing and stumbling. Out from behind him shot a fluffy white cat — and then out darted Bum!

The two cats ran into the woods by the lake, not slowing until the brutal incandescent glow of the house was far behind them, and the only light came from the pale reflection of the gentle moon on the lake. "We're never going back," Bum said.

"No," the fluffy cat, whose name was White Girl, agreed. "Never."

"Ahem," Carla said to get their attention. "Bum? I'm Carla, and this is my power animal. We've come to take you back to your true self."

The young, sleek and handsome Bum drew back and bared his teeth. "I'm not going anywhere without White Girl!" he growled.

Carla turned to the white cat. "White Girl, you can come too. Would you like that?"

"Yes, please, get us out of here!" she said in a breathless tremolo. So Carla scooped up both kitties, and they rode the osprey up into the sky, setting down again at another place, even lonelier than the woods by the lake, where snow-covered train tracks crossed each other beside rusty buildings, and a group of men in grease-stained coveralls stood around a fire

78

burning in an oil drum. One of the men walked to the edge of the circle of light cast by the fire and chucked a paper bag of food scraps into the shadows.

Then all of the feral cats came running, a motley assortment of lame and diseased creatures, among them Bum and White Girl, older now, their coats dirty and their bodies thin. Quicker than the rest, White Girl cornered an empty tuna fish can and hungrily licked inside the rim. Its sharp, jagged edge cut into her muzzle, but she was too hungry to stop eating. Gingerly, Bum approached her, meowing and reaching forward with a scarred paw. White Girl hissed at him, laying back her ears, and he backed down. He watched her dig into the tuna can without another thought for him. He gave a long, wounded howl, then slunk away out of sight, dissolving into the shadows.

"Gather up these lost souls as well," the osprey said solemnly. "You will take Bum's soul parts home, and I will take White Girl's lost soul parts back where they belong." Carla did as the great bird bade her.

"I have them all here," she said. "But they are anxious even now about being separated. They are very sad and very sorry. It is so painful." Her voice caught in her throat. "I wish there were some way..."

The bird bent his graceful neck and stroked the small, trembling cats' heads with his long beak. "Tell them they will see each other again someday, Carla," he said in his hushed baritone. "There will be plenty of time for them later, when they each return to the ever place."

And so Carla returned Bum's lost and wandering soul parts to his newly mended body, and she and Amber sent him home to Deb, who had, indeed, rediscovered her own compassion in caring for this broken, unlovable creature. To Deb's delight, her faith was rewarded when Bum's body and soul recovered and his true sweet nature began to emerge at last. You can be sure, though, that Bum continued to wear the scars of his many battles of the claw and heart like the proud badges of courage they were.

This poor kitty! When he came to Deb, he was just recovering from a severe bout of coonhound paralysis, which had compromised his lungs. Deb's veterinarian also said that newly hatching heartworms were clogging Bum's lungs, arteries and veins. The vet didn't expect Bum to survive, but she gave him a shot of antihistamine to reduce the inflammatory reaction to the invasion. Even if he survived this bout, she indicated, he would surely die in the next attack.

He didn't. In fact, since Bum's shamanic healing session four years ago, there hasn't been another heartworm. Deb says it's a miracle. I thank the spirits for their healing and blessings.

— Carla

I've been grrrreeeeaaaattttttt!
Oh, what's wrong with dying?

Marcus in the Ever Place

One thing seems certain: human beings are about as good at understanding dying as parrots are at playing the piano. As Debra's cat Marcus knows too well, sometimes we just struggle and struggle with it. Here's the low-down from a hardheaded feline with some good advice for members of the "challenged" species.

A sunny day just isn't complete without a few animal-shaped clouds floating dreamily overhead, don't you think? The sky above Amber's cottage was home to a rollicking litter of tiny white kittens the day Carla arrived bearing a letter from Debra that contained a bittersweet request. Deb was a nice lady from Texas who had been mistress to any number of happy cats ever since she was a little girl. Naturally, some of these cats had grown old and passed on, while still others had arrived. But there was one cat whose death had never sat right on Deb's conscience, and that was her favorite kitty, a tabby named Marcus. A powerful — some say arrogant — personality, Marcus had grown moody and aloof while Deb was busy packing up her household for a cross-town move. In the commotion, Deb failed to recognize Marcus's unseasonably bad attitude as a symptom of grave illness, and she was totally unprepared when he crept off somewhere and died alone. Deb had never forgiven herself for being so distracted when her cat had needed her most, and now she wanted Carla to find Marcus, wherever he was, and apologize to him.

"Hello?" Carla called, opening Amber's squeaky front door. "Anybody home?"

"I'm in the kitchen!" Amber called out. "Come on in, I'm cooking up something delicious!"

Carla followed the smell of beef hearts simmering in garlic and found Amber mincing ingredients in a green ceramic bowl decorated with blue fish skeletons. "A little kale, a little ginger," Amber said. "A sprinkling of ground flax seed — that's the secret ingredient. And we'll top it off with some of my home-baked kibble — croutons for cats."

"Sounds yummy," Carla said.

"Well you can't have any," replied Amber. "It's for Marcus."

"I see you're a step ahead of me," Carla said, grinning.

Amber held up a spoon coated in gravy. "I am also behind you all the way. We spirits can do things like that. Now let's find that kitty while this grub is still hot."

"It's been several years since Marcus died," Carla said, following Amber out onto the porch.

Amber nodded thoughtfully. "He could be hard to find. For this trip, I think we'll take the convertible," she said, holding open the front door and snapping her fingers. A rectangular Persian prayer rug with a pattern of red, green and gold trees and chalices shook itself awake, leapt up from the hall floor, and came to rest in mid-air beside Amber, its fringed edge curling upward like the lip of a fancy toboggan. "Give me a leg up, darlin', would you?" Amber said over her shoulder.

"You got it." Carla laced her fingers together beneath Amber's sandaled foot and easily boosted her onto the carpet, where she settled herself into a kneeling position, careful all the while not to spill the contents of the green cat bowl on her white gown.

She turned to Carla and offered her hand, lifting her into the pillion position. "The Persians really had it right when they wove these magical sleighs, and I was so lucky to have this one choose me at the gift exchange at the Golden Temple several moons ago. It was a great party, you should join me sometime." Carla was about to say that she would love to, when the carpet lurched forward making her grab the edges just to stay on. With this she realized that she might be too corporeal to be admitted to such a divine party. There in the third layer of the Upper World, the carpet swooped down to carry them close along the ground, slowing, searching, gliding, and finally coming to rest on a patch of grassy turf.

"Aha!" Amber said to Carla in a stage whisper, pointing toward a small hillock with a hole in it. The opening was overhung by long tendrils of grass and assorted tree droppings. "Methinks there lies a den of catness. What do you thinks?"

Carla was about to answer when a gust of warm feline breath rustled the twigs and leaves at the entrance to the shady den, and a gorgeous, full-grown tabby tom cat rolled out into the fresh upper-world daylight, twitching his fluffy tail into a questioning S and blinking his large marigold eyes at Carla and Amber. After taking in their presence, Marcus's eyelids fell to half-mast. He dipped his body into a long stretch, digging his front claws between the blades of spring grass and kneading gently, then he yawned so deeply that Carla would have slipped away into her own dreams if Amber had not whispered, "Well, introduce yourself".

"Hello, Marcus," Carla said, refocusing on her purpose. "My name is Carla, and this is my friend and teacher Amber. We're here to help you."

Marcus looked Carla over and gave out an arch, patronizing sigh. Then he looked at Amber. She blinked her eyes heavily in greeting, the way cats do. Marcus smiled. "I don't need any help," he said easily, then broke into a grin. "But I'll take the food, thank you!" His tail twitched at the end of each sentence like an exclamation point.

Amber placed the food dish between his paws, and while he bent to eat his meal Carla couldn't resist stroking his sleek back. He raised up his butt to meet her hand the way cats do. "Now go down to the base of my tail and scratch ever so lightly," he ordered. Carla complied. Marcus leaned into her hand and stamped his back feet, purring madly. "Ooh! That is so nice!"

"So Marcus," Carla said. "How have you been?"

"I've been grrrreeeeaaaattttttttt," Marcus purred with so much pleasure that Carla wondered whether some of the greenery growing around the mouth of Marcus's den might not be catnip. "I live here in this nest."

"Are there other kitties in the nest?" Carla asked.

"There's one," Marcus replied dreamily, "she's a black and white long-haired cat." Then, in the way cats do, he shot Carla a vivid picture of his life with the black and white kitty. "Ah," Carla said. "She's your mother!"

"That's right!" Marcus declared, with all the satisfaction one would expect of a kitten who had finally gotten to have his

86

mother all to himself for as long as he wanted.

"Marcus," Carla ventured. "I've come because Deb is a little unsettled about your passing and she wanted me to discuss things with you and see how you felt about it."

Marcus paused to lick the last trace of gravy out of the dinner bowl, then sat down and started to groom his whiskers with his paws. Finally he asked casually, "About what?"

"Well, she was concerned that she wasn't giving you much attention because she was so busy moving."

"Yes! All that packing was very bothersome! And it was scary. Going to a new place is very scary, and I didn't want to do that, so I died."

His answer was so abrupt that Carla almost let out a bark. "You're very clear on that, huh?"

Marcus rolled onto his back and watched a bumblebee swizzle through the air, casually swatting at it with his paw. "Oh, what's wrong with dying?" he said lazily, "Let me tell you how it is for us cats: we make contracts when we come into the world. And part of our contract is that we can get out whenever we want to. I was miserable, I felt bad and I didn't want to go to a new house, so I got out. See?" Marcus shrugged.

He rolled back onto his haunches. "Believe me, you don't want to live when you feel terrible. Life is not about lying around feeling terrible. You don't go to earth to be sick; you go to earth to play, to have a body, to eat delicious food, to sharpen your claws and stuff. When it gets to the feeling miserable time, you think about leaving and coming back home."

Carla glanced at Amber, who just smiled softly, reflecting his wisdom in her eyes.

"It's funny," Marcus went on. "When you're on earth, you think about people leaving you, but when you're up here and someone you love goes to earth, you think about them leaving you here. It's all the same." He looked deeply into Carla's eyes. "You understand that, don't you?"

"Actually, Marcus, I've been around here enough that I do understand it," she said.

"Why don't you stay then?" He said teasingly.

"Because I'm not dead yet," Carla replied. "In fact, I'm not even sick."

"Right!" Marcus cried. "So you better be enjoying yourself!"

"I'm trying to, honey," Carla said ruefully, "I'm trying."

"Good!" he declared.

"Deb is concerned that the hustle bustle of the move made you feel abandoned, so you went off to die alone." Carla ventured. "That's an unsettling feeling for a human being. Can you help her with that?"

"Yeah," Marcus said, shrugging. "I went to die alone because that's the way it's done. That's the ritual. Whenever cats can, they prefer to die alone — as you call it. In reality, we die in the full company of the spirits that love us, of our families, of our ancestors, and of all the spirit beings that are with them." He sighed. "People die that way too, of course, but you just don't see it, so you get anxious. People are like those folks who hang on a train — you know what I'm thinking of — people trying to say goodbye at a train station, the person on the train is squished up against the window as the person on the platform runs after the train saying "Goodbye, goodbye, goodbye!" Marcus sat up prim and sphinx-like, marshalling all of his catly dignity. "We cats say goodbye when the person boards the train. I kissed Debra goodbye before I went off to die."

"It's hard for her to understand that," Carla said.

"Because she couldn't see all the spirits that were with me, like Mommy!" Marcus said, growing tender and kittenish again. "But if she could have, she would have known I wasn't alone, that it was just time for me to go to my new family — my old family — my other family.

"Tell Deb not to cry! And tell her that toward the end it was very hard to show love and compassion in a body that felt so terrible, and I'm sorry if her soul was hurt by my passing. I'm deeply sorry." He sank into a pleasant memory and smiled, purring conspiratorially. "Can I send her a private message?" he asked. "Will you give it to her?"

"Of course, Marcus."

"Tell her I want to lick her toes. I want to chew on her toes again."

Amber giggled behind her hand. "Oh, I'm sorry, that's just so sweet!"

"Deb still loves you very much," Carla said. "Can I read you a bit of what she wrote to me?"

"Yes," said Marcus, "Please do!"

"She wrote: 'He was very special to me. I raised him from a little furball.'"

"Yeah, it was fun!" Marcus said, the delight of the memory flooding his face. "I used to try to suckle her finger. And I loved to cuddle near her ear."

"I'll tell her," Carla said, just as Marcus's black and white mama came stretching and yawning out of her den and gave her full-grown kitten a clawless box on the ear. Marcus rolled on his back, inviting play, but she ignored him, swishing her tail like a grand dame dismissing a servant with a flick of her fan. She sat down in the sun and began to carefully lick her paws while Marcus gazed after her in tranquil, contented bliss. He seemed to have already forgotten that Carla was even there, and Amber gave the nod.

"Goodbye, beautiful kitty," Carla whispered as she and Amber mounted the carpet for the return journey. "Bye, Mama Cat."

Back at the cottage, Amber parked the air-freshened carpet in the hallway, and walked Carla to the gate. "That Marcus is all cat," Carla declared.

Amber just smiled. "Let's just say that he won't be coming back as a parakeet any time soon."

Deb's reaction to this session was pure relief. After the session, she told me how she remembered one day when she was making her preparations for the move, and she distinctly heard Marcus say, "I am not moving with you." But she didn't know what that meant. This journey made it clear. It's so hard for us to know the boundaries of our obligations as caretakers. Marcus, though, was very clear about it, and he showed us that, in the end, many cats are indeed their own keepers.

— Carla

You will only experience your power, and your light, through the bond you make with your person, Krafla. You must show Mary how to love. That is your job.

Krafla's Tears

When I first met Mary's rescue horse, Skip, he was
basically schizophrenic. One moment he was soft eyed
and sweet, and the next he was a killer, literally trying
to eliminate any human who came near. A beautiful
chestnut thoroughbred gelding, Mary just knew he was
a nice guy deep inside. Our first session was an hour
and a half marathon. I found the disincarnate spirit of
a stable hand hiding inside him. The guy didn't even
know he was dead, but he sure as heck wasn't going to
let anyone get him. He would take control of Skip's body
and lash out with hoof and tooth. It was a process, but
we coerced him into coming out and going to the angels
for healing. Then we labored over Skip, adding layers
of empowerment and healing to restore his balance
and happy disposition. The healing lasted for several
years, with Skip becoming gentle and easy to handle.
But there was something about Skip that made it easy
for intruders to latch onto him. Periodically, Mary
would call me for follow-up if Skip became ill, or if his
behavior regressed.

For this session Mary asked me to help Skip with
some backsliding, and to also work with her Icelandic
mare, Krafla. Krafla kept trying to bite people, highly
unusual behavior for this amicable breed, and she was

anti-social with the other horses, even the other Icelandics,
which was equally remarkable. Mary just wanted to help this
poor mare be normal and happy.

When dogs or horses need help, I turn to Kay, a Native
American healer whose log home lies in the Lower World, a
shamanic realm that's rich with earthy magic. If cats thrive
in the airy, infinite reaches of the Upper World where Amber
lives, then dogs and horses are by nature creatures of the vivid,
visceral realm below, where infinity is best captured by the
inward gaze.

For certain journeys, Carla abandons the elk and maple
hoop drum in favor of a larger one made from the hide
of a bear. Its sound is sonorous and slow, and it makes
her steps heavy and sure as she circles the reflecting pool,
preparing for the journey to begin. Raising her rattle, Carla
sang a low song into each direction, repeating the plea for
assistance, beckoning the unseen ones to come closer, to
surround her and guide her path. When finally she felt them
on her, a wing brushing her shoulder, a wet nose touching her
hand, she was ready to go below and find Kay.

From the outside, the way to the Lower World looks like
the burrow of a small, furry animal — a fox or a prairie dog
— but just past the narrow entrance, the tunnel turns into a
sparkling passageway paved in raw turquoise and quartz. You
may have noticed the shaman's fondness for long, peculiar
passageways between one realm and the next. Think of it this
way: you are reading a book (maybe even this one), absorbed
in the story, when just outside your window your dog barks
— you look up, startled, to watch him tree a squirrel. Can you

describe the passageway you traveled through to get from the world in the book back to the world you live in? The journey was probably instantaneous — yet weren't you left with a vague sense of vertigo, a sense of having been ripped too quickly from one dimension into another? In Non-Ordinary Reality, where time and distance are fluid, getting there is always as important as the place itself. There's a reason shamans call their practice journey work.

Descending, Carla made her way though the jeweled cavern, down to a pool where she always paused to bathe, washing herself clean of the earthly preconceptions that may have clung to her like burrs on a saddle blanket, muddying her vision and making her second guess herself. Shaking herself dry like a dog, she headed out across a rocky landscape towards a tall escarpment. The uneven flight of stairs set into it weren't visible until she reached them, a steep upper course carved out of the cool rock by her ancestors long ago. At the top, she clambered over a last flared outcropping and stepped into the dazzling bright sunlight of the Lower World.

The way from here crossed an open plain of tall, brittle grasses that stretched to the horizon: a blanket of ochre rising to meet the turquoise sky. After a while, the grasses dwindled to prairie scrub, becoming almost desert-like as she headed into a sculpted stone canyon that narrowed before opening out again to reveal a fertile river valley. Kay's log house lay here, just across a shallow running creek, occupying a dusty patch of ground between two corrals and an open fire pit, and facing a clearing of sacred space, a healing circle.

The deerskin that served as a door to the circular hut flapped open, and Kay emerged, stooping to shoulder his way through the low opening. How he managed to stand at his full height inside his house Carla had always wondered – she'd peeked inside on a couple of occasions, but the cabin was too much of a bachelor pad for the purposes of entertaining, and they usually visited sitting on the circle of logs ranged around the fire pit, where Kay served her burnt coffee with chicory or velvety Mexican chocolate with a pinch of cinnamon and salt. Carla was an avid student of horsemanship, but for every tip she learned in a weekend training clinic in Ordinary Reality, Kay offered a dozen lessons that were richer. He survived repeated lifetimes because of his intimate partnerships with equines, his swift legs in storms, battles and hunts. There is a deep seated trust that builds in the bones of this kind of person, a trust any equine recognizes, an unstated commitment to do right for one another. Carla depended on Kay for all things horse, and most things doggy too. Dogs just naturally hung out around the place, and Kay was equally adept at helping the dogs Carla brought to visit him. But today was a day for two horses who were emotionally wounded, with no external scars to show for it. Carla began to explain her purpose for the visit, but there was no need. Coffee would have to come later this trip.

Kay already had things ready for Skip, who was running circles in the far corral, the place where a good deal of serious healing work was done. Kay's appaloosa companion, Star Spangled Banner, had heard Carla's call and had gone to fetch Skip before Carla even arrived. Kay carried a burlap sack filled with green-topped carrots, bits of damp earth still clinging to them, and he passed Carla a handful of small, rosy apples to stuff into her pockets. Skip was a regular customer, and Kay knew exactly the approach to take.

The ground in the arena was covered in a thick layer of moist sand, which obviously made Skip feel like prancing. Carla settled onto a stool in the middle of the oval and waited for him. He approached her, nose stretched forward, nostrils flared, then he bucked, kicked and ran off again. "Just wait," Kay said, a smile curling at the corner of his lips as he watched the horse lunge and snort this way and that. Kay wore buckskin pants and a leather vest over his tanned chest. His hair, which could be short or long depending on his mood, hung down his back in a glossy sheet. Carla had once asked him which tribe he belonged to, and Kay had raised an eyebrow and shot back, "Which lifetime?" Carla would appreciate that reply when she was probed with questions about her own heritage and training. But it also left her a little confused as to who's ancient traditions she was learning from this cross cultural savant.

Carla pulled out an apple, casual as could be, and took a noisy bite out of it.

Skip's ears shot forward, and he stopped himself mid-prance, wheeling around. "What's that?" he asked, trotting up and stopping just out of range. "Can I have some?"

"Mmm," Carla said around a mouthful of succulent apple pulp.

"Say, is something wrong with me?" Skip asked anxiously. "Is that why they called you?"

Carla swallowed. "Why do I make you nervous, Skip?" she asked innocently enough.

"Because you make me change," Skip said. "And I don't like that."

Kay whistled. "What don't you like about it, Skip?"

"It makes me have to do more," Skip said petulantly. Carla could see Kay's lip twitch as he repressed a smile.

"Do more of what, Skip?" Carla said, acting puzzled.

"Going around in circles," Skip said, tossing his head. "I don't like to have to go 'round in circles! Before, I used to get away with stuff, and now, thanks to you, I can't."

Kay strolled around to the right, so that Skip was left standing between them. "I dunno, Carla, what do you think?" he asked. "Do we make Skip go around in circles?"

"Oh no, Kay," Carla said. "I think we helped Skip get more comfortable in his body. That's what I remember."

Kay nodded, stroking his chin. "That's what I thought, too. Skip, do you remember when you were afraid all the time?"

"No," Skip said sulkily. "I don't remember anything like that."

"Ah," said Kay. "You don't remember why we visited you last time, you just remember that things changed?"

"Well, yeah!" Skip said.

"It's funny, the way we learn," Kay said, addressing Carla now, right over the top of Skip's withers. The horse dipped his head and snorted at the sand. "When we can't remember the bad, we don't know how good we have it. You know what, Skip? You're alright!"

"I am?" Skip's head shot up.

"Yeah," said Kay. "You don't need anything at all. We're not going to do a darned thing to you. In fact, I don't know, I think I'll just keep this bag of carrots. Come on, Carla, let's go."

Carla hopped down from her stool and followed Kay toward the paddock gate. Skip followed along beside them. "Where are you guys going?"

Kay grinned at Carla, then reached into the bag and handed her a carrot, taking another one out for himself. "Say, you

98

want a carrot, Skip?" he asked.

"Well, yeah!" Skip said.

"You going to tell us what's going on?" Kay asked.

Skip hesitated, sulking. "I'm not sure how it will help me."

Kay stopped and turned to face Skip. "I can promise you only one thing, and that is that I love you and I want to help you. If I help you, your life can only be better, not worse. It means you feel better physically and happier emotionally. That's why I'm here, Skip. I'm not here to hurt you."

With this, Kay set down the bag of carrots and turned away again, leaving Skip to his thoughts and his snack.

At the healing circle, Kay built a small fire, then burnt some offerings — a handful of leaves first, some juniper berries, and a bit of lichen. "Spirits, make rain on this horse so he understands," Kay said softly, crouched beside the fire. "Spirits make wind on his horse, so he understands."

Extinguishing the fire with water from an oilskin pouch, Kay stood, satisfied. "Now we wait." He and Carla sat in the cool shade of the doorway to the barn in companionable silence. Skip, meanwhile, had polished off the bag of carrots and was now sniffing at the sand disconsolately. Then he took to running in circles. Suddenly, he stopped and rolled in the wet sand, then lunged to his feet again and shook himself violently. A bee buzzed up and perched itself on his withers. It walked up his mane and crawled right into Skip's twitching ear.

Kay leaned over to Carla. "See that? What the bee is whispering to Skip right now is: 'I could sting you, but I won't because I'm your friend and I want to help you.'"

Then Skip called out across the paddock to where Carla and

Kay sat. "Hey, you guys!" he said. "You know, I have this stone in my right front foot. And I think that if you still wanted to, maybe you could help to get it out."

Expressionless, Kay walked up to Skip and ran his hands down the horse's right front forelock, lifting up his hoof. He pulled an iron hoof pick out of his pocket and freed up the stone. Then he picked up each of Skip's hooves in turn and cleaned them out with the iron pick. While he worked, a string of silent visitors arrived, by ones and twos and threes, surrounding the corral, some riding bareback, others leading their ponies by the reins. These were Kay's compatriots, Indian braves whose numbers reached all the way to the sky, as far as the eye could see, there were so many of them.

Skip watched them arrive, but said nothing. There was no hope for any creature to harbor anger in its heart around them. Any trace of anger was totally overwhelmed by their power and strength. It was imperative. They were imperative. They were the power of the imperative.

"There you go, Skip," Kay said, lowering the last hoof. "That is much better, isn't it?"

Skip stood on the hoof and sighed. "What else can you do for me?" he asked almost sheepishly. "To make my life better — as you say?"

Kay patted the horse's neck. "Skip, you're a magnet for things that don't belong to you. You just need to be cleared out. Kind of like what we did the last time. And every time we clean you up, you become less and less attractive to the things that don't belong in you." Kay gave him a slap on the haunch. "That, and I want to adjust your spine. That's going to change you, too."

Skip looked over at Carla. "What's she going to do?" he

asked warily.

"She will work with me," Kay said.

"I'm ready," Skip said. He lowered his head and opened his nostrils wide.

Carla and Kay joined hands, and as the horse sucked in his next breath, they slipped right up his left nostril, along with the air.

The inside of a horse's body is a velvety place, like the ocean on a hot planet where the primordial soup is rich with nascent life. Carla felt the soft pressure of the horse's throat envelop every inch of her, buoying her up and relieving her of the pressure of gravity. A sharp, tangy metallic smell filled her nostrils. She would not need to breathe. She swam forward, alongside Kay, and as they squished forth into Skip's belly, she became aware that they were not alone.

Kay took a small bundle of herbs from inside his vest, sage from the desert mixed with a black ironwood branch and rabbit brush, and lit it. Carla heard a gurgling, then a scuffling, a mutter and a shriek, followed by a sudden sense of calm, and a marked reduction in temperature. Whatever had been hiding out in the horse's belly had fled.

"That takes care of that," Kay said. "The braves have taken it away. It will not be back." He ran his hands along the lining of Skip's stomach. "He may have some worms, too. Tell Mary to check for worms. His left hind leg appears to have some tenderness along the cannon bone, between the hock and the fetlock, maybe a ligament." Kay put healing power into the horse's leg, then followed it up to where the hip joined the spine. Kay lay a small, round stone there, and its pressure seemed to relieve some of Skip's pain, for his posture shifted. The stone filled a void, like the missing keystone to a crumbling arch, and suddenly Skip stood taller, his feet rooted to the ground. A column of energy shot up through his hooves and spine, jetting through the crown of his head and exploding upwards, connecting him to the land and the sky, like a fountain, or a tree.

Carla and Kay slipped back down the horse's moist snout, growing as they tumbled out, until they stood again in the paddock. The braves, sure enough, had gone. "How do you feel, Skip?" Carla asked.

Skip stood very still, listening to his insides. "Alone," he said curiously. "But it feels good. I want to sleep."

"That's good, honey," Carla said, stroking his neck. "You sleep, you rest."

An albino bat fluttered down out of the sky and danced in the air around Skip's head, promising to stay and protect him. Skip's eyelids drooped. "I'm going to sleep now," he said thickly.

"Goodnight, sweetie," Carla cooed. She turned to Kay. "I think it's time to go see what's happening with Krafla," she said.

Kay paused. "Krafla is an Icelandic horse; before we approach her we'd better pay a visit to Sleipnir. He may be able to help us." Carla's bones thrilled at the idea of visiting the high, cold plain where Sleipnir's herd of rugged Icelandic horses roamed, her spiritual home in the Upper World.

Kay put his fingers in the corners of his mouth and whistled sharply, and Star Spangled Banner came cantering toward them from somewhere on the open plain. Named for the bright starbursts that dappled his haunches, Kay's Appaloosa was both friend and spirit guide, an expert healer in his own right. He danced to a stop, arched his mane, whinnied like

102

an opera singer and tossed his shapely head twice at Carla in greeting.

"And where's the black fur ball today?" Star Spangled asked jokingly, referring to Carla's own Icelandic horse, Kolur.

Carla smiled. "Oh, I expect he'll be along any second, now that you're here."

Sure enough, a speck of dust appeared on the horizon, gradually resolving itself into little Kolur, his stocky legs pistoning along at a flat out gallop. Carla loved to watch him run. Kolur skidded to a stop beside her and snorted. He'd barely broken a sweat. Accustomed as he was to cold and altitude, he found movement in the warm, low regions almost effortless.

"It looks like we're all here," Carla said.

Together, horses and riders lunged skyward. The trip was far, and it took but an instant, the horses' hooves churning upward through the many layers that lay between them and the icy fiords of the Upper World, a place of wooly Norse horses with powerful legs and huge, muscular hearts. Their leader is Sleipnir, Odin's sometimes steed, and he appeared before them now, all eight of his stocky legs beating the icy tundra.

Sleipnir is the essence of pure power, the embodiment of joy in strength. He is a simple, ancient, primitive creature, equal parts muscle, bone and spirit. He is in constant motion.

"Sleipnir," Kay said, "we've come to ask you a favor?"

"What?" the great horse snorted, great arabesques of white steam curling from his nostrils. "Do you need another mare?"

"No, precious," Carla said. "One of your mares needs your help. Krafla, another little black horse like this one. She's very

103

unhappy. She bites people, but I believe it's because she is very sad."

"Of course," Sleipnir said. "Don't you know why? She's crying because she's lost a foal."

"Oh," Carla said. "That does explain things. Can you help restore her foal to her?" She knew that he could, but Sleipnir was not one to coddle the weak. "She'll have to come here and ask me for it," the horse said. "And she has to come on her own."

There was no arguing the point. "This is a challenging day," Kay muttered, as they left.

Now, instead of returning to Kay's ranch, they rode down through a secret opening hidden in the clouds, down into the Middle World, to the snow-covered farm outside of Albany, New York, where Krafla munched molasses-soaked grain from her bucket.

"Krafla," Carla called, edging Kolur up beside her. The two black horses could have been twins. "I've come with a message from Sleipnir, the leader of our herd. I know you've lost your foal, and that this makes you very sad. Sleipnir can help you, but you must go to him."

Krafla lifted her head from her bucket and rolled her heavy-lidded eyes toward Carla. She looked so disconsolate that she might barely make it to the water trough, let alone the far reaches of the Upper World. Yet a small spark flickered behind her eyes, a flash of blue that hinted at untapped reserves.

"How do I go there?" she asked in a small voice.

"Look up," Carla urged her, "look up, Krafla, breathe out, and follow your breath. Breathe, and follow your breath, yes, breathe and follow your breath, higher... higher. You're

104

climbing there, now, climbing! When you get there, remember to call out to Sleipnir. He will come to you."

Carla and Kay watched Krafla drift up, up, up, becoming a miniature figure against the white sky. They heard her whinny in the distance, then watched as Sleipnir rocketed across the dome of the sky toward her, followed by a herd of gangly-legged foals. He circled, nuzzled her, checking to see if she was in heat — ever the roué, that Sleipnir — and nudged her toward a black and white foal that immediately fell to suckling. The others surrounded her, butting her flanks with their muzzles.

"These are all your children," Sleipnir said. "They are here, and this is where you belong. I'm just letting those people down there borrow you for a while — Mary and Alex. You have a job to do. It's your job to show them the power of your light."

Krafla looked at him in bewilderment. If ever a pony appeared to be a creature of the dark, it was her. "Where is that power supposed to come from?"

Sleipnir laid his muzzle on her chest and blew the power of love into her heart. "The power is inside you," he said. "The next foal you have will be mine. You can have it up here or down there, it doesn't matter, but it will be mine. But you will only experience your power, and your light, through the bond you make with your person, Krafla," Sleipnir explained. He flashed her the image of his human partner Odin riding him, a merged pair in body and soul "You must show Mary how to love. That is your job."

Krafla's spirit floated back down to the snow-covered stable, carrying the love of Sleipnir partnered with Odin in her womb and in her heart. Carla and Kay greeted her as she settled in the pasture.

"Feeling better?" Carla asked.

Krafla gave a frisky kick and tossed her mane in answer. "I have brought back the power of Slepnir's and Odin's love to give to Mary," she said with pride.

"That's wonderful," Carla said. "What is it, Krafla?" she asked, sensing some consternation.

Krafla glanced warily at Kay and crept closer to Carla, as if she wanted to speak woman to woman. "Do you think..." she began, and paused, and Carla could have sworn she had just seen a black horse blush. "Do you suppose she'll get pregnant, too?"

Carla laughed. "If she does, the world would be better off, wouldn't it?"

"I suppose so," said the horse.

"And Krafla," Carla suggested, "do you think you might find it in your heart to share some of that love with Alexandra, too?"

Krafla shied. "Well, no — no, he said it was for Mary."

"Try it with Alex, too," Carla said firmly but gently. "I'll bet that there's enough love to go around to every person you care about."

Krafla snorted and shook. "I don't care about people!" she whinnied. "Oh, well, oh well, oh — maybe I do. Maybe I do care!" Distraught, Krafla began spinning in circles, then stopped, wavered and sank to her knees. "Maybe I do! I don't know! I don't know!" Huge sobs shuddered through the horse's body. "I don't know! I just wish somebody would stroke my mane, just touch me, touch me..." She broke off, unable to continue.

106

"Krafla, honey," Carla said, kneeling beside her and stroking her mane while she continued to quiver and sob. "Honey girl, that's what love feels like! And it isn't bad to have. It feels like that when it first starts coming through you, but after that it begins to feel like a beautiful rose opening on a spring morning. It feels like dewdrops on the grass, moist and delicious in your mouth. It feels like going into the hay barn and eating all the hay you want. It feels like running free in the pasture after you've had your saddle taken off. It feels like sun radiating down on your back after it's been chilly out. It feels like all these things. That's what love feels like. You share that. You share that with Mary, and you share that with Alex, and you can let a lot more of it stream through, because the power of love is as great as the universe itself."

And where Krafla's tears had flown, a small trickle of emotion opened up, a steady flow that soon began to pour through her, until the heaving sobs subsided, and her fear and distress gave way to wonder.

"That's it," Carla cooed as Krafla stood again, on legs as shaky as those of a newborn foal. "That's it, now. Steady, girl."

In 2000, Skip crossed over and joined his favorite spirits for recreation in blue grass heaven. But he still visits Mary regularly, thanking her for her love and blessing her with his pure joy.

Krafla did stop biting Alex and Mary, but she did not get pregnant. I finally met her in person not long ago, and she was happy to meet me, and very sweet.

— Carla

Trailing along in the gale generated by
its mighty wings followed a flock of
tiny angels.

Junkyard Jesus

With a broadly muscled chest and a head like Hephasteus' anvil, the Rottweiler has the outward appearance of a vicious and imposing beast. When roused, its full-throated bark is enough to rattle windows and turn your garden-variety burglar's knees to jelly. Yet contrary to what some people think (and in the case of the burglars, let them not be disabused of this image), Rottweilers are most often gentle creatures by nature, loyal and devoted cuddlebugs who consider themselves to be lap dogs - often to the consternation of their petite female guardians, let me tell you. A favorite with children, for whom "Carl" or "Mattie" is often more of a pony than a dog, the Rottweiler is truly the perfect family dog.

Brenda's three year-old Sara, however, had a personality that ran against type. Kind and lovable as a puppy, she had grown more and more surly, and had lately taken to snapping at strangers and even family members. Brenda had been advised by her vet to put Sara down, and she called me in a last-ditch effort to save the dog.

Sara the Rottweiler was in no condition to travel, which is why Carla and Kay went to meet her in her own back yard on the outskirts of Chicago, accompanied by various and sundry of their spirit helpers, including a coyote, a bear, and a magnificent cormorant. The suburban back yard was large and generous, covered in a thick pelt of well-fed grass and bordered by a high wooden fence so recently put there that the boards still smelled of the forest. In the center of the yard, a tremendous elm tree spread its branches like a giant umbrella, shading everything and providing a symphony of birdsong.

Poor Sara, however, took no pleasure in the serenity of her environment. Despite her idyllic surroundings, she moped disconsolately and mustered nothing but a surly glance for the spectral entourage that now approached her.

The spirits conferred, whispering their consensus.

"Her right side and left side are not integrated properly."

"And there's that spirit clamped on to her. It's an ancestor!"

"Its teeth go right through to her DNA..."

"Hereditary..."

"We'll have to work on transfiguring that."

"The spirit must be helped, too."

"There are techniques..."

The spirits fanned out in a circle around the doghouse. "Sara," Carla sang out gently. "Oh, Sara."

No response.

"She wants to be called Rosie," Kay said. "That may be the name of the ancestor."

Carla held firm. "Sara, my name is Carla, and I have come

110

all the way from Oregon to speak with you."

Sara raised her head. "Where's Oregon?" she said crossly.

"Good question," said Carla. "I live a long way away. I've come here as a spirit. I've come with my teachers and my friends to help you."

"To help me with what?" Sara said.

"Brenda has asked us to come."

Sara laid her head back down on her paws. "Is she angry?"

"I don't know if she's angry," said Carla, "but she is upset and concerned."

Sara sighed through her nostrils. "Then she is angry."

"That possible," Carla conceded. "But the key issue is that she is worried. There is a difference, you know."

"I can take care of myself," Sara said. "Why should she worry?"

Carla smiled. "I think in part because you take care of yourself too well."

This annoyed Sara. "What do you mean?"

Carla took a step toward Sara and kneeled down. "She says that you have tried to bite people recently."

Sara curled her lip. "They were bothering me!" she snarled. "They were trying to touch me, to get near." She shot Carla a warning look.

Carla smiled. "Don't even think about trying to bite me, girl!" she said. "It won't work. Here take a chomp."

Carla waved her hand in front of Sara's face. The dog lunged and snapped, but her jaws closed on nothing.

Carla laughed. "See? It doesn't help. We are in this together."

Sara was intrigued – and all the more suspicious. She sat up and looked squarely at Carla.

"Brenda says that you have been increasingly aggressive, and that you seem to be unhappy and in pain. She would like to try and relieve that pain, and she would like to heal whatever it is that makes you feel aggressive so that you can live in harmony in the world." Here Carla paused and her kind expression turned grave. "And so that you can stay here in this place, quite frankly."

"What do you mean?" Sara barked.

"I mean this," said Carla, "and I will be blunt with you, Sara, because you are a blunt kind of dog: There is no place in Ordinary Reality for dogs who bite people. That's it. Dogs who bite get put down. So your options are very simple. You can work and try to heal, be filled with love, or you can try again in another life. Those are your choices."

Sara turned away. "I don't have to listen to this."

"Unless you want to be a guard dog and lead a life of viciousness," Carla continued. "We could also request that you become a guard dog in some tacky store someplace, what do you think of that?"

Sara looked at her, suddenly with an altogether different gleam in her eye, and when she spoke the voice that came out of her body was harsh as a tractor scooping up a load of gravel: "I think that is what she was meant to do."

Carla nearly jumped out of her spiritual skin. Even the cormorant flapped its wings as if blown back by the sudden burst of anger. "Who are *you*?" Carla asked.

The dog who wasn't Sara bared his teeth. "I'm Jesus!"

"Strange name for a dog," Carla said.

"You damned well better believe it!"

Now we're getting somewhere, Carla thought. "How did you come in here?" she asked politely. "Where did you come from...Jesus?"

"Saint Dominic!" he growled.

"Excuse me?"

"Saint Dominic. In the Virgin Islands."

"And just how did you end up in Illinois?" Carla asked. "Tell me that, Jesus."

He lowered his head and leered at her, the hair on the back of his neck bristling as a low growl built in his throat and a film of red descended over his half-lidded eyes.

"Okay, I believe you!" Carla said. "I believe you." She paused, giving him time to calm down. "Jesus, do you know what you look like?"

He snapped at the air an inch from her nose. "I look like a mean mother *&^$%!"

"Yes you do," Carla said, waving away a gust of his hot, nasty breath. "You most certainly do! But do you know what you look like to me?"

She paused, but he held still. She had piqued his curiosity.

"A Doberman Pinscher. You're a Doberman, isn't that right? Ahhhah! A Doberman attack dog." Carla saw the spirit of the Doberman illuminating through Sara's Rottweiler skin.

She could tell by the flicker of pride in his eyes that she was right. "Yes, you're pretty good at that, huh? Were you pretty good at that, Jesus?"

"The best!" he said.

Carla cocked her head. "How did you die?"

"What do you mean?!" he barked.

"Jesus," Carla explained evenly, "you are in the body of a Rottweiler. Look at this dog — is that you?"

Jesus chuckled. "No, but she's getting tougher every day. She's learning."

"I know," Carla said, "though it makes her miserable and unhappy."

Jesus rose up to his full height and shouted: "*It makes her tough!*"

Carla smiled sadly. "It may make her tough, but it is going to get her killed," she said. "Then where will you be?"

Jesus swung his massive head back and forth in restless agitation. "I'll have another dead dog! I don't care! I can find another shell to take over."

"Jesus, are you in pain?" Carla reached out toward him, but he flinched away from her touch reflexively, as if her hand were a tongue of flame.

Carla glanced at Kay, who nodded. "He was beaten as a puppy," Kay said quietly. "He was beaten with a pipe."

Jesus whimpered. "You okay, Jesus?" Carla asked. "I'd like to help you heal that pain. Would you like that? Would you like to be happy again? You can be. The way out of this pain is to come with us to the light and find love. Do you remember love, Jesus?"

The big, angry dog cast her a look of genuine befuddlement tinged with fear.

Carla nearly gasped. "There is no memory of love in this dog at all!" she whispered to Kay.

The two of them stepped back, rejoining the circle of animals. The snake raised its tail and began to rattle, while

114

the cormorant spread its wings and began a rhythmic beating, whipping the air in the yard into an electric frenzy. Alarmed, Jesus began to bark, and Carla sang:

I call on the angels to come for this dog!

I call on the power of my spirits to come for this dog!

Gusts of wind began to beat down on them all, like the wind generated by the blades of a helicopter as it lands. Carla sank to her knees under its force, and it was all the poor dog who at once was both Sara and Jesus could do to keep on barking. A winged figure descended out of the sky, a great, reptilian beast with scaly wings, crusty, armored hide and wild red eyes. Its hooves and wings pounded furiously. A rhinoceros. Trailing along in the gale generated by its mighty wings followed a flock of tiny angels the size of sparrows.

"Jesus, do you see this animal here?" Carla called out. "He's coming to help escort you. He's going to take you to the place where you can understand your aggressiveness, where it can have its right place within the context of love. He knows more about it than you do, Jesus — you got it from him."

The rhinoceros opened its beaky jaws and plucked Jesus right up by the collar. The chain that held it snapped like a string. And the great, crusty angel-creature bore Jesus away, home to a place where only the fiercest die and are born, and where anger such as his is smelted down again into love — not a place where mere mortals or shamans can easily follow.

"Sara?" Carla called gently to the soft pile of dog that was left behind. "How are you doing, girl?"

She lifted her head. She looked different, a bit hollow. Kay gathered her up in his arms, and the cormorant bore them away across the land, swooping down, through the earth and out again into the bright sunlight of Kay's ranch, where it was springtime. Kay laid Sara's prone body gently in the shallow waters of the spring. She lapped tentatively with her tongue, then thirstily. She laughed, then rolled, stood and shook herself vigorously, then bounded off across the grass, snapping the heads off the wild coreopsis, nasturtiums, lavender and lambs' tongues that grew along the creek bed, all plants that would help to further her healing.

"There is still a void in her right side," Kay said. "We need to do a soul retrieval for her."

Carla called to Sara, while Kay went to make the necessary preparations. When he returned carrying a bowl of steaming soup, the big dog lay with her head lolling in Carla's lap. "This soup has magic healing in it," Kay said, setting the bowl down before her. The rich meat broth was full of beef bones and carrots. Sara thanked him, and lapped it up greedily. Kay caught Carla's eye and nodded; she climbed on the cormorant's back and took off, skimming the landscape of the Lower World in search of Sara's lost soul parts.

The first thing they found was a whimpering puppy. Her eyes weren't even open yet, and she couldn't find her mother's milk. Bolder siblings, older by minutes, pushed her away with their little paws. "Oh little one," Carla called. "Come now, to three-year old you, where you can eat beef stew. Come now." And she gathered up the baby pup, which slipped neatly inside her body for the trip home. The mother Rottweiler turned her head to look. She thanked Carla and asked that she take the puppy back where she belonged.

The second soul part Carla found was a young whelp sitting quietly by herself, driven out of Sara's young body by the pain of a wrenched shoulder. "Would you like to come back to yourself now, and help Sara heal?" Carla asked. The pup nodded eagerly and jumped into Carla's belly to keep

116

company with its younger self.

The third and last soul part Carla discovered pacing back and forth next to its body, which was racked with the pain of a raging bladder infection. "Why doesn't it work?" the young dog said in frustration, giving the prostrate body an angry little kick, just like a person pounding on a vending machine that has eaten change. "Why doesn't it work the way it's supposed to?"

"I can help you," Carla said. "But you'll have to come with me."

The frustrated dog gladly hopped aboard, and Carla bore all three of her charges back to where Kay waited with Sara beside the creek. Kay shook his rattle while Carla extracted the lost soul parts from her warm belly and blew them into Sara's chest one by one: *Whooosh! Whooosh! Whooosh!*

The voids in Sara's body filled, which pleased Kay. "I can see a whole dog now," he said.

"Yes," said Carla, "but would you look at that?" She pointed to the distinct pattern of bite marks on Sara's shoulder, where the dog that was her ancestor had taken hold of her. "I don't think Jesus is the only one taking Sara for a joyride."

Carla knew that in order to get the ancestor to release its bite, the one responsible for the disruption to Sara's DNA and the bulk of her physical ailments, she would have to find it in its own lifetime, and heal it. So what did she do? She reached out where the bite marks glowed hottest and grabbed the animal right by the throat. Hanging on, she felt around for the thin thread of time that tethered it, and finding it, made her way hand over hand to the place where the dog had died.

She found herself in a cage in the back of a truck — a dogcatcher's truck. "Why do you cling to Sara?" Carla began, but the dog, Rosie, didn't even know she was dead. "Never mind," Carla said quickly. "Let me take you to where you belong. Where is it that you want to go? No, not into the Middle World, with Sara. Let me take you to the Upper World where all your ancestors are. You are dead, my friend, and it's time for you to move on. Here, let me break your connections to this world." One by one, Carla snapped the threads that bound her to time and place. "That's quite a bladder infection you've got," she said evenly. "It must hurt quite a lot." The dog replied that it did. "You won't have to suffer that pain anymore," Carla assured her, "and neither will Sara." Carla lifted Rosie free of the illusory cage in the back of the truck and turned her over to the sturdy band of angels who would bear her away to her Upper World home.

By the time Carla returned, Sara was sound asleep. Carla ruffled the big dog's ears gently until she stirred. The big bellows of her chest worked in, then out. "I can breathe!" Sara said. But she could hardly keep herself awake. "This place, it's so peaceful and quiet," she murmured.

"Something tells me it's going to be a lot more peaceful and quiet in Chicago from now on, too," Carla said, but Sara was already asleep.

I did the session for Sara on a Sunday, but it was a while before Brenda called me back after getting my email report on the results. After the healing session, Sara lay around for three days. On Wednesday afternoon, Brenda looked over at Sara, and she knew she had returned from Kay's healing circle. "Sara was back," Brenda reported. "I looked at her and there was a

golden glow around her, and her eyes were sparkling. I said, 'She has come back.'" Frank — Brenda's skeptical partner — also saw it and said, "What is with Sara's eyes, is she back?"

"Sara stopped biting, and she has never tried to bite again," Brenda continued. "She still can have her moments, but she has never tried to attack a person. It's a miracle. I was going to have to put her down."

Brenda said that Sara's shoulder stopped hurting after the healing work, and her bladder infection went away. She went on to say that everything that went wrong with Sara always happened on her right side, where I had seen a void. She says that now the right side is fine. I feel blessed to have been able to connect Sara and Brenda with the compassionate healing spirits.

— Carla

"Aw, crikey," said an English boxer. "That ain't Perseus Magic, that's Pan Gu."

Mighty Pan Gu

Victoria may be the sweetest woman on earth, and she is blessed with dog friends who grace her like white butter cream on a perfect cake. When I met her she was struggling to save her dear Shar Pei, Perseus Magic, from a congenital disorder. I spent many hours in Non-Ordinary Reality helping Perseus Magic with his effort, and then when the struggle was over, helping him settle into his new home in the Upper World. It took Perseus Magic some time to determine when and how to return to Victoria. He packed his suitcase, but he couldn't get clear on exactly when and where to jump back down to earth. Finally, Victoria and I knew he had been reborn, but she still couldn't find him! Then the breeder she had been working with, and whom we identified as the one who was most likely to rebirth Pan Gu, decided that she would give Victoria a very special pup. Such a blessing is often a sure sign of the right soul. {My magic horse Kolur was gifted to me} But Victoria wanted me to give her the final word on her new baby's lineage.

Sometimes, big dogs come in small packages, and Pan Gu is a Shar Pei who sometimes thinks he's a lion — a friendly lion, mind you. But does this recent arrival know what became of Victoria's previous companion, a little dog named Perseus Magic?

As Carla climbed down into the Lower World in search of a funny little dog named Pan Gu, whose owner thought he may or may not be the reincarnation of another equally funny little dog named Perseus Magic, the first thing she heard was the distant sound of combat: the fierce, rumbling growl of a bear or a lion engaged in a battle over feeding grounds. From the smallness of the roars and bellows, Carla guessed that the argument was taking place far in the distance, a dispute over territory way beyond the borders of Kay's ranch.

By the time Carla crossed the creek and entered the healing circle in front of Kay's house, she could see that what she'd taken for the sound of a very large lion far away was in fact the sound of a very small dog close by. And the only dispute in evidence seemed to be between the dog and Kay's sleeve.

Kay was sitting on the dusty ground in his buckskins, a delighted grin lighting his face as he wrestled with a creature that, at first glance, appeared to be a wadded-up, furry blanket with teeth. The little animal grabbed a mouthful of fringe on Kay's sleeve and set his weight back, growling deep in his throat and shaking his whole body to and fro. Kay laughed, and cuffed the little dog with his free hand, sending him sprawling end over end. He landed legs akimbo, then immediately sprang up and bounced back for more. When he stopped and shook himself, his loose skin waggled to and fro. Two beady, bright, round eyes stared up at Carla expectantly, and his little mouth opened in a panting grin, while his pink petal of a tongue curled up in a smile. He looked like a little

122

Chinese lion with folds of jiggling, furry yellow skin for a mane.

"This is Pan Gu," Kay said, dusting himself off and proceeding with the introductions with all the solemnity he could muster — which wasn't much, since it was impossible to behold Pan Gu without smiling. "Pan Gu, this is Carla."

"Pleased to meet you," Carla said. "I've been sent by Victoria to communicate with you. Would that please you?"

"Yah!" Pan Gu yapped.

"If you wouldn't mind," Carla continued, "I'd like to slip inside your body so that I can see the world from your point of view."

"Looks like he's got room for you in there, with all this extra skin," Kay said fondly, ruffling Pan Gu's irresistible folds. The little dog leaned into him.

"I'd like to visit your home and see how you live," Carla said. "Would you like that?"

"Yah!" Pan Gu yapped again. "Sounds fun! Yarf! Garrr! Do it!"

So Carla slipped inside of Pan Gu's body and looked out through his round eyes. "Oh my goodness!" she cried. "I'm — why, I'm *enormous!*"

She took a few steps, feeling the grounded solidity of his thick, bandy legs, the power of his wide, open chest surging forward against the pressure of a harness and leash. A big black dog with floppy ears looked back at her with a gentle, quizzical expression. Ah, let me at 'em! she thought with gusto, as Pan Gu's little motor revved up, rumbling at full-throttle. I'll show 'em who's the biggest dog around here!

The leash pulled her back across a cool, green lawn, and a

pair of arms enfolded him, enfolding him. Aaaah! The feeling was indescribable as Pan Gu's body melted into the crook of an arm, held firm, now rocking back and forth with the gentle vertigo of a swinging hammock. A hand scratched his neck, all five fingers digging down between the folds of skin and everything tingled. Aaaaaahh! That's nice!

"Down you go!"

Carla felt them running, now, across the succulent green lawn as the liquid, radiant heat of the sun made Pan Gu's yellow fur molten and warm. Their spine stretched into a joyful arc with every wide-open stride. What's that up ahead? It's raining diamonds! Bright, clear jewels falling from the sky. They hit their back, exploding in coolness. Rufff! Yarrr! Garf! They ran back and forth, snapping at the bright, glittering drops, catching them in their mouth where they immediately turned to liquid.

Victoria called from the back door, and Pan Gu left the sprinkler behind, bounding up the steps. A cat with long orange and white fur sat on sentinel duty on the porch rail. The cat's back arched as Carla passed, more in annoyance than alarm. "She always looks at me like that," Pan Gu thought to Carla with regret, "as though my very presence were the end of the world!"

"I would like to be your friend, you know," Pan Gu said to the cat.

The feline just hissed. "You can't possibly mean that!" she said archly, dismissing him with a violent flick of her tail.

Pan Gu barked once for good measure, and went to find Victoria. She was sitting on the couch reading, and he hopped up beside her, nosing up under the crook of her arm. Dogs, cats, sprinklers — nothing was as good as this, slipping off to

124

sleep in the warm, soft, comfort of Victoria's embrace...

Carla stepped out of Pan Gu's body just as he drifted off into that state of doggie twilight between wakefulness and sleep, the alpha state where dogs spend so much of their time. "That was fun!' she said. "Thank you."

"Rarf!" Pan Gu said, jumping up. "My turn!"

Carla laughed. "You want to jump inside me? Alright, come on in."

Pan Gu jumped inside Carla, and the surged to her home in Oregon, Pan Gu sitting tight in Carla's skin.

She ranged around the rambling farm house, showing him the kitchen, the office, the yard, the bar. He was fascinated by the horses, three rugged Icelandic ponies who stared back at him warily. They weren't fooled for a minute. "Do you think I could sit on one?" Pan Gu asked.

"I don't see why not," Carla said. She led Kolur, the black one, over to the paddock fence and used it to give herself a leg up onto his back. Kolur stood stock still while Pan Gu surveyed the world from horseback, but a moment was all his patience could stand. Kolur is a funny horse, very compassionate and gentle, but Carla alone is his mistress and others aren't always welcome aboard. And Pan Gu's claws through Carla's skin were just too much for him. "Get the dog off me," He said through clenched teeth. "Get the dog off me!"

Carla hopped down, and let him go, and Pan Gu leapt back into his own body.

"Well," Kay asked him, "how was it?"

Pan Gu shook himself. "Tight," he said succinctly. "Garf! And your feet are so far away from your hands. How ever do you keep track of your whole self? It must be terrible to be so — so discursive!"

Carla laughed. "Sometimes it is, Pan Gu, sometimes it is."

Kay smiled and winked at her.

"So," Carla continued. "Pan Gu, what do you know of Perseus Magic?"

"I don't know," Pan Gu barked. "Who's that?"

"Well," Carla said, "you're in your body, so you probably don't know. What we really need to do is go find Perseus Magic and ask him what he has to do with you. Would you like to go on a journey?"

"Uh huh!"

Carla, Pan Gu and Kay set out on a trail that began 'round back of the house and climbed up a short hill to where the Tree of Life grew, its massive trunk disappearing from view high overhead as it shot through the roof of the Lower World and rose on up, where its leaves and branches unfurled to become the many levels of the Upper World.

"This is where we'll find him," Carla said, craning her neck skyward. "If he's where I last saw him."

"You don't expect me to climb that, do you?" Pan Gu said.

"Naw," said Kay. "We're taking the elevator."

Kay ducked into a cleft in the base of the tree, and Carla and Pan Gu followed. Inside, the three of them were able to stand comfortably, though it was close and dark and smelled of moss, mushrooms and termite dust. "Next stop, the land of dogs," Kay said, scooping Pan Gu up with one fringed arm and putting the other around Carla's shoulder.

Up they went, rising with slow majesty, gathering speed as they went. Through chinks in the massive trunk they caught

126

enticing glimpses, first of the lands of the Lower World spread out below them from ever more dizzying, unimaginable heights, then of the discrete, jumbled regions of the Upper World, a magical hanging garden of infinite variety flashing past them in all the colors of the known universe.

Suddenly, they slowed, and Kay led the way again, out through a crack in the fragrant bark and onto a sturdy branch surrounded by a riot of autumn leaves. They gamboled along its swaying length and out onto a broad, russet-colored leaf that quickly became a desert beneath a red sky, then a series of flame-colored canyons at sunset. The canyon walls were pocked with hundreds of caves and burrows, home to spirits of dogs who wait to be reborn.

"Excuse me," Carla said to a pack of mid-sized ruffians playing catch with a well-chewed, sun-bleached bone, "I'm looking for a little dog who goes by the name of Perseus Magic. Is he here?"

The dogs paused at their sport. A collie spoke up. "Uh, lady," he said in a voice that harked to at least one lifetime spent on the Eastern Seaboard, "you're standing right next to him." He lifted his chin in the direction of Pan Gu.

"Aw, crikey," said an English boxer. "That ain't Perseus Magic, that's Pan Gu."

"Jeez Harry," said the Collie. "Perseus Magic, Pan Gu, what's the difference?"

Pan Gu was busy sniffing and exploring around the group's perimeter. He looked up at Carla, puzzled. "Have I been here before?"

Wordlessly, a sad-looking Weimaraner with gray around his muzzle dragged a round, soft-walled dog bed over to Pan Gu and dropped it at his feet. Pan Gu sniffed it, then climbed in and curled up. He knew it was his.

Carla caught Kay smiling, with a twinkle in his eye. Not many people knew that Kay had dimples — only when he visited the land of dogs. "Kay," she said, "Can you help us all understand how this dog can be both Perseus Magic and Pan Gu? Could you maybe tell us a story that will help us understand a thing like this?"

Kay perched cross-legged on a rock and the dogs gathered 'round, tails wagging. Still others poked their heads out of their burrows along the cliffs, and the canyon became an amphitheater. And the dogs were all so quiet that Kay barely had to speak above a whisper to be heard.

"Once upon a time," he began, "there was a star that shone extra bright. Its beams reached out across the land and hit the window of a small house. There was a stirring inside the house, and a door opened and out came a cat.

" 'Meowhat?' he asks of the star, 'What?'

"The star reached down and grabbed the cat and took the cat up to itself." 'I want you to help me find a dog named Perseus Magic,' the Star said.

" 'Where?' asked the cat.

" 'Wherever you look to find him,' said the star.

" 'Meowkay,' the cat agreed.

"A cloud came. The cat caught onto it and flew, sailing over a forest to land in a grassy yard. He sniffed the ground and walked around, and he saw a Shar Pei. Pan Gu! He went up to the dog and asked, 'Are you Perseus Magic, or do you know where I can find him?' Pan Gu barked at him, 'I'm Pan Gu!'

"The cat said, a bit disbelievingly, 'So you say!' And he looked up to the star and sent the message 'I've found him.'

"The star was pleased. 'We sent him out with his suitcase,' it said, 'and we were not sure where he landed. We'd lost sight of him for a bit. There is a thickening layer that the spirit crosses through as they come to earth. He went through the thickest part. He does not recall who he was. And that's okay.'

"The cat wanted to return to his home in the house, but the star said 'No, you must stay down here and watch out for this one.'

"So the cat does watch out, but not with fondness; rather, with a sense of duty."

Pan Gu's eyes brightened in recognition.

"So you see, little one," Kay said fondly, "that's who you are. But I suspect you won't remember it... even as we take you back down now."

As they said goodbye to all the dogs and made their way back thought the canyons, across the desert and up the branch of the great tree, Kay explained to Pan Gu how he, too, had a mission, just like the fluffy orange and white cat did. "You have special work to do, little one," Kay said, "for your person, Victoria. Your job is to hold her heart and keep her emotions in reason. That is to say, you will explain to her why things are okay even when they feel that they are not."

Pan Gu smiled and said, "Rrr-yes!"

"You will do it very well, my friend."

As they sank gently back toward the Lower World, Carla asked, "Kay, what gifts can we give these wonderful ones, Pan Gu and Victoria?"

Kay reached into a beaded pouch that hung from his neck and extracted a small, polished stone; And then he reached out into the ocean and gathered a beautiful crab. Cupping his hands, he blew it into the stone: *whoosh!* "The crab says he will give you the power of his cleverness, wisdom and protection," Kay told Pan Gu.

"And I can take the hard knocks!" the little dog barked.

Carla heard a beautiful song in the breeze. Kay reached out and gathered it in, then blew it into the stone. *Whoosh!*

He then retrieved the image of a landscape, the power of the seashore with a little varmint diving into the sand, and birds flying over the waves. The whole scene was one of joy and honesty. *Whoosh! Whoosh!*

And finally, Kay blew love from his heart into the stone, and pressed the token into Carla's palm — something to take back to the Middle World.

"Welcome home boy," Carla said as they stepped from the tree back into the circle of Kay's ranch, running her fingers through Pan Gu's neck folds. Before they left, Kay tied a white ribbon with red polka dots around Pan Gu's neck, and gave him a little polka dotted scarf for Victoria. "I'll take him home now," he said.

"And I'll take this," Carla said, holding up the fist that held tight to the precious stone. She held onto it, even as she crossed the creek and climbed through the tunnel hung glittering with quartz and turquoise. She held it tight as she bathed in the warm waters of her sacred pond, and she still held it when she opened her eyes in her office.

In a few days, Victoria would receive a note from Carla in her mailbox, along with a bit of polished stone from Kay.

A happy ending. This session confirmed Pan Gu's identity. Just like he was as Perseus Magic, Pan Gu is a complete delight. Pure love in doggy flesh.

— Carla

APPENDIX

The Tools and Techniques of Shamanic Healing

What is Shamanic Healing?

Shamanic healing is the most ancient form of medicine, as old as mankind. Shamanic images have been found in the earliest cave paintings, and most, if not all, tribal cultures' traditional healers find their power in shamanic traditions. A shaman crosses at will between the world of Ordinary Reality and into the world of the spirits, enlisting compassionate spirits' help for healing and to gain knowledge. To do this, a shaman enters a trance-like state, which Michael Harner, founder of the Foundation for Shamanic Studies(1) and author of *The Way of the Shaman*, calls the "shamanic state of consciousness." (2) Shamans often employ a steady rhythmic sound to enter this other realm, which Harner calls "Non-Ordinary Reality", and meet spirits first hand.

While each tribal culture has its own particular shamanic rituals and traditions, there are commonalties in most shamanic cultures. Michael Harner has identified many of these elements and teaches them to modern people in a series of workshops offered by the Foundation. He calls these practices "core shamanism" because they are central to most shamanic traditions, yet exclusive to none. The basic tenants of core shamanism are:

Entering the Shamanic State of Consciousness — A person can enter the shamanic state of consciousness and cross into the realm of the spirits by listening to a steady drumbeat and consciously focusing on a series of steps in his mind. The experiences the shaman has in Non-Ordinary Reality are just as real as those in Ordinary Reality, but of course, they are different.

Working with Spirit Allies — The shamanic practitioner has individual spirit allies who guide his path in Non-Ordinary Reality. These compassionate spirits provide information to the shamanic practitioner for himself and his clients. The shamanic practitioner asks the spirits to diagnose and heal illness, both emotional and physical, and to help clients overcome difficult situations in their lives. Power animals and human spiritual teachers are common allies. Some shamanic practitioners work with ancient gods and goddesses as well.

Addressing the Spiritual Causes of Illness — The spiritual component of illness is caused by one or more of three conditions: loss of power, loss of soul and/or intrusion by a spiritual entity that doesn't belong in the client and is detrimental to the client's well being. The spirit allies can diagnose and heal each of these conditions, but the role the shamanic practitioner plays is critical in enabling the connection and healing to occur. The practitioner is the hollow bone who allows the healing power to come through. They direct the work through their request and intention, and enable it through compassion. ◉

Spiritual Power Loss
Loss of power occurs when we have undergone some

trauma, or when our power is sapped from us though circumstances or intention. We have all experienced feeling physically drained from effort or stress, and the powerlessness that can go along with it. Spiritual power loss is similar, but the power doesn't come back after a fine dinner and a good rest. Spiritual power loss leaves us feeling weak to our core. It can manifest as feeling unlucky, trodden upon and depressed, as if we have a black cloud over our heads. Some people with power loss are accident-prone and hopeless. Life can feel more like a struggle than a fun game.

Where does this spiritual power come from? And how can we be disconnected from it? How can we build power in ourselves to help us remain strong and effective on our life's journey? The sources are as infinite as the spirits themselves. Each living being is connected to a web of spirits who love it and support it. Some are power animals, the spirits of animals who have crossed over and who seek to share their wisdom, strength and compassion with us. Our ancestors often wish to connect with us and lend power and aid. Some are the spirits of plants with whom we feel deep connection. Spirits of places, of structures and other elements can also be important power sources for us. Each time we break a connection with a power source, we risk losing our power supply. Accidents and events can disconnect us, leaving us helpless. Fortunately, the loving and compassionate spirits want to help us restore our power, and even to build more of it. Shamanic practitioners reconnect people and animals with their core power sources, restoring physical and emotional well-being.

Animals certainly experience power loss. Horses who undergo a dramatic illness such as colic can suffer power loss. Dogs who have lost a beloved guardian may become deeply depressed. Abandoned cats often are suffering from power loss. Even moving can cause some animals to feel disconnected from their source. I make it a standard practice to retrieve a spiritual power source for each client animal. To deliver that power to them, I blow it into their bodies just as Sandra blew my soul parts and power animal into me. Early in my career, I had a client ask me to help her poor dog, who suffered from deep fear of thunderstorms, and who was a nut about barking at anything he heard in the street. The dog, Jake, lived behind a firm wooden fence, so he couldn't see what was going on outside. He could only hear it.

Jake told me that the reason he was afraid of thunder was because once, in a storm, a tree branch had fallen on him, and he was terrified it would happen again. We did healing work around the event, bringing him back the part of his soul that had separated from him when the branch fell, and that helped a lot. But the major healing came when we reconnected him with a power animal. This powerful spirit took on the role of being Jake's eyes and ears. He would fly out over the road to see what the noises were and tell Jake if it were appropriate to bark, or if it were nothing. And he promised Jake he would protect him in a storm so that trees would never fall on him again. Jake's guardian reported that he became much quieter and calmer after the session, and really grew quite reasonable about dealing with the uncertainties in life. ◐

Soul Loss

Loss of soul occurs when we undergo a trauma severe enough that part of our soul disconnects from the rest of our being, often for self-protection. This is similar to power loss, but is often experienced as a disconnection from one's own self. The soul part stays fixed at the time of the event, but in Non-Ordinary Reality. Often, soul loss results in loss of memory or a feeling of incompleteness. This disengagement makes it easier to survive traumas such as accidents, abuse or emotional disturbances. Children can suffer soul loss from events that are traumatic to them, but may seem trivial to adults. Soul loss can also occur when another person "holds" onto a part of us, and doesn't let go. (An old lover, perhaps.)

Once the traumatic event is over, complete healing can occur when the missing soul parts are returned. The shaman facilitates this event by journeying into Non-Ordinary Reality and, with the help of spirit allies, finding the missing soul parts and bringing them back home. Then there is a period of integration, during which the client gets to know the returned soul part(s) again, and together they work to heal the old wounds. This often takes several months.

Many other forms of therapy can also achieve soul part return, and certainly people experience spontaneous soul retrievals as they do personal healing and growth work. Shamanic intervention, however, can bring dramatic and rapid results; like a strong wind in the sails of recovery.

Animals also experience personal soul loss, but not nearly as frequently as people. Perhaps is it their resilient natures, or their more inherent connectedness, but I have found that maybe a third of animals I treat need personal soul retrieval. They have usually suffered intentional abuse, a sudden shock or severe conditions. I have found, though, that herd and pack animals can suffer soul loss from being disconnected with their spiritual or physical groups.

I have known several Icelandic horses, usually those exported from Iceland, who suffered depression or anxiety disorders when they were separated from their large herd families. When I reconnected their spiritual selves with the spiritual Icelandic herd, the horses underwent strong and rapid personality changes. One of them is my husband's horse,

Elmar, who was imported into a large farm in Canada where he lived with a herd of Icelandic horses. We brought him to our farm, where his only companion was a dominant Peruvian Paso gelding. Elmar started out with a stiff upper lip, but over a few months, his attitude eroded. In a shamanic journey for him, I asked my teacher to explain the problem and solve it. He showed me that Elmar was disconnected from his collective soul, and that, while the ideal solution would be to return him to a herd of Icelandics, we could achieve strong results by reconnecting him with the spiritual heard of horses from which he came, and to which he will return when he passes.

It was an amazing session; my first experience of merging with the herd of horses who are part of my own blood (you can see that I really have four legs when you look at me from the right angle). We took Elmar's spirit to the herd, led by Sleipnir, Odin's eight-legged mount, and he merged with it. They became one being—a single, many-legged horse. Then they became individuals again, and Elmar's now-healed spirit returned with me and re-entered his body. Elmar changed immediately; he became a gentle riding horse again, and was far more cooperative. The smoky look in his eye shifted to a gentle softness. And he began to get along much better with the Peruvian.

When we ask the spirits to help, we are often graced with bounty extending far beyond the session itself. In this case, a few months after the session, we received an email from the horse farm in Canada offering us a horse as a gift. Kolur, a 13-year-old Icelandic gelding, was having issues that made him unfit to sell, but the farm thought he would be a good fit with us. He was also one of Elmar's best old buddies from the farm, and as it turns out, my spiritual partner. A gift from heaven indeed! With Kolur's coming, Elmar's sense of security was completely restored. He remains a perfect horse, and my husband's best friend. ◉

Intrusions

When a person or animal suffers power or soul loss, intrusions can enter the resulting "holes" in the spiritual body. Intrusions are really just spiritual entities that are where they don't belong. Everything has its place and purpose. When something that doesn't belong there is lodged in us, it can make us quite ill. Intrusions also result from anger directed toward another, or toward ourselves. (Be careful what you think and say, for your thoughts and words have the power to inflict harm!) When the spiritual component of illness is healed, the physical component can quickly heal as well.

Intrusions are the most common problem I see in my work. Most serious illnesses have a spiritual intrusion component. Intrusions are common, and they can prevent other forms of healing from sticking. Lameness, nagging localized pain and energy blockage are often caused by intrusions. Sometimes, when the intrusion is removed, the problem is solved completely. Other times, the problem can finally be resolved through a "normal" course of healing and the application of other treatments.

Intrusion can be quite blatant, or it can be subtle. The story in this book of Sara illustrates the most extreme example of an intrusion — she was sharing her body with the disincarnated spirit of a junkyard dog who wasn't even fully aware that he was dead. The dog was making poor Sara crazy! More common are intrusions that are not as identifiable, but cause localized pain or illness. Horses who have mysterious and persistent lameness often become normal again after a shamanic session of extraction and power retrieval work.

A jumping horse named Ricky whom I worked on was very stiff picking up the canter to the right, and even would give little bucks of discomfort in the canter. His guardian had addressed all the usual suspects: saddle fit, chiropractic and so on. In my journey, I rode Ricky and felt his discomfort and saw the intrusions in his chest area and right hip. He showed me the event where they had come in. A few years back, he had crashed into a fence and hit the ground pretty hard on his hip, as well as bashing his chest. While his body had healed, the intrusion that had entered him left him feeling residual stiffness and discomfort. I removed them, and got information from the spirits on follow-up things that the guardian could do, like massage and stretching exercises. Soon, Ricky moved fluidly again.

Intrusions often accompany cancer. A sweet mare had skin cancer invading her face from her eye to her ear. Her guardian didn't want to put her down, but wasn't getting much hope from her veterinarian. She asked me to help, and she asked the vet to do one more excision of the tumors. It worked. I removed the spiritual intrusion associated with the cancer, extracting it from all the places in the horse's body where it had taken root. The vet cut out the physical cancer, and the horse has completely recovered.

Sometimes, intrusions can be quite subtle. One of my horses, Jark, stepped on a nail in his left front foot. It entered the frog from the rear and poked upward about two inches. The x-ray showed that it had just missed penetrating into the area of the foot where infection becomes quite dangerous. My vet and I were thankful that the prognosis was very good. Of course, I asked the spirits to give him complete healing, and I am sure they were instrumental in his rapid and easy recovery. But the intrusion for this example wasn't in the foot itself. One evening as I was soaking Jark's foot, I connected with the spirits to bring him healing power. They showed me an intrusion in Jark's shoulder area, and said it was quite painful. I extracted the intrusion and put it where it would be restored to its proper place in the world. As I put my hand back on Jark's shoulder, I heard a big crack as the bones readjusted. Jark let out a big sigh and fully relaxed. It makes sense that he would have tweaked something, as he favored his injured foot. As a shamanic practitioner, I saw that injury as an intrusion, and removing it was the thing that allowed the body return to normal. ◉

Protection

This work can be dangerous. Most notably, the entities that cause illness can move out of the client and into the practitioner. Other dangers lurk as well, and an unprotected journeyer can become a sick person rather quickly. To guard against these things, I have learned to call upon my spirit allies to protect me. I never travel alone in Non-Ordinary Reality. I am always seeking the compassionate spirit allies' advice and perspective, and most importantly, I ask them to directly protect me from any danger that may arise. ◉

The Non-Ordinary Reality Roadmap

I teach how to journey to the Middle World in my introductory workshop. Participants begin by traveling in their mind's eye to a special place in nature, and then experience that place with each of their senses. I then retrieve a unique power animal for each participant, and they meet that animal in their special place in the Middle World. All of our working the in the introductory workshop is done in the Middle World, for it is easy to communicate with animals there.

In many shamanic traditions, the world tree links the

worlds. The roots burrow down to the Lower World. The trunk is in the middle, and the branches stretch up to the Upper World. I see this tree quite distinctly in my travels, and in fact, I use it to find reference points. One of the many lands of dogs is several main branches up the trunk in the Upper World, off to the left, or west. Everyone sees Non-Ordinary Reality in his or her own way, however, the Foundation for Shamanic Studies is undertaking a grand research project wherein each participant in the three-year training program creates a map of the worlds in which they travel. Seeing dozens of these hanging side by side, the continuity between maps is said to be amazing.

While most do, not every shamanic culture recognizes the three-part layering of Non-Ordinary Reality. The Celts, for example, travel only in one land; to them, it is all the same. Indeed, in my travels I have found it easy to move between levels, almost as if they were one. But I also have found that shamanic work is much stronger when a practitioner knows where they are and can map their path.

Understanding the levels is instrumental to understanding the landscape. In my advanced trainings, I teach people to explore each world, recognizing its distinctions. That way, they can find allies in different places, and can set their intention to go to one place or the other, and know where they are at all times. ◐

Key Tenets of Shamanic Practice

One Spirit

There is no hierarchy of being. If each individual is a continuum from individual self to the one, then each is also equally sharing in oneness, and each is on par with all others. Indeed, I have seen that humble ants have as much wisdom as profound human sages when I connect with them along the continuum. Thus, in my view, man is not the keeper of the planet's life forms, but a very active participant among many equally important and interdependent beings. We may be the ultimate tricksters — in mythology, tricksters are the often troublesome, but essential, agents of change.

With no hierarchy of being, a cat is not superior to a mouse, nor a man to a horse, and so forth. We do seem to have interdependent and archetypal relationships that are critical to the balance of the world. For example, I have found that the spiritual power animal for a prey animal, such as a horse, is often its predator, such as a lion.

By embracing the concept of one spirit we let go of any superiority complexes that can prevent us from truly understanding another being. This notion is similar to the revelation I had in horse training when I learned that listening to the horse on all levels was the secret to mutual cooperation. TTEAM training introduced me to this notion, but Clicker Training drove it home. Using the clicker and positive reinforcement, we ask the horse to do certain things that we want, and we reward him for those actions. We ignore unwanted behavior and remain focused on noticing and rewarding the behaviors we seek. The result is that the horse's mind is turned on, fully and happily engaged, offering us the behaviors that make both of us happy. In fact, our animals are training us in exactly the same way when we interact with them. My old lab Sammy does a dance to remind me to give him his morning egg. When we settle on behaviors that are mutually pleasing, we have a partnership, often with shared responsibility and power.

In shamanic animal communication, the concept of one spirit opens the door to revelations that are rarely

142

experienced by those with preconceptions of our superiority. Because mankind's superiority is a central tenant in many church doctrines, embracing the notion of one spirit is challenging for many people. In my workshops, I ask people to suspend those belief systems for the duration. Later, they can reflect on the experiences they had and find a personal point of view that is comfortable.

Intention

Intention is our roadmap through Non-Ordinary Reality. Clearly setting intention allows us to experience those things that are important to our mission, and to accomplish our tasks. Intention connects us with the correct animal. Intention shifts our focus from one issue to another. Intention is our concentration, our way of manifesting what we are seeking.

Intention, backed by determination, may be the most powerful tool we have in life. In my work I set my intention in advance and repeat it out loud as I begin each session. When I teach, I repeat the intention for each journey three times, and then sometimes even remind people of it as they are engaged in the sessions. Intention helps us stay on track. Shamanic animal communicators learn to trust that their Non-Ordinary Reality experiences are real and are related to the mission they intended.

Sometimes, intention is the only means I have for knowing I am on track. I did a session to connect with a dog who had recently crossed over. Zenda was a beautiful greyhound whose guardian missed her terribly. Typically, when I go to find the spirit of an animal who has crossed over, I move quickly into the Upper World and connect with the correct spirit. Not this time! I was carried off by my power animal on a Middle World expedition that seemingly had nothing to do with the task at hand. It was really fun, I have to admit. I toured the Himalayas and went shopping in Kathmandu, where I found a very unusual rug. Throughout, I kept restating my intention to find Zenda, and the spirits kept replying that I was indeed on course.

Finally, they took me to the top of a Himalayan peak, and we lifted up into the clouds and to the Upper World. There, though, I still couldn't find her spirit. All I could see was a great expanse of clouds. I felt an immense sense of deep peace. Where is she? I asked my teacher, and he replied, "She has ascended." I got it. She had transcended even the memory of having a body and had merged with the universe. It felt very Buddhist and wonderful. There is a secret I learned from Celtic Shamanism of a magical pool where one can call up the images of spirits, and they will appear in the water. Thinking that she might manifest for me there, I went to the pool and asked her to appear. It worked! She explained that she was in bliss and that her love for her mother would radiate through the clouds themselves and perpetually fill her with love. I thanked Zenda and returned.

I have learned to trust that the information the spirits give me is perfect for the guardian to hear — but this one was so unusual that I was a bit concerned delivering the news. Her guardian wasn't a bit surprised! She had actually schooled Zenda in the practices of Tibetan Buddhism, the religion she herself practiced. She was delighted to hear that the lessons had taken root, and that Zenda had transcended so beautifully. I have to say that I was pretty relieved — and amazed at the depth of the experience on many levels. I am looking forward to going to Kathmandu someday in Ordinary Reality and finding that wonderful rug!

Compassion

Intention sets the direction, but compassion supplies the power to accomplish the mission. The compassion and love of the spirits motivates them to reach down and help us through our dramas and traumas. As a shamanic practitioner, I beg them to show compassion for animals and people who are in pain, and they do so, without judgment, giving help at some level, subtle or profound.

Our compassion is critical as well. Animals open up to us when they sense we care. We can call on the loving compassion of the spiritual world to come through us and flow into animals and people when we do healing work for them. Shamanic practitioners are trained in specific techniques for calling in and applying the healing power of compassionate spirits. We become like a series of transformers, stepping down the intensely powerful compassionate source of universal love. The compassionate spirits can connect with it more directly than we can, embodied as we are in our individual selves. Linked with their spiritual allies, shamans help direct that power into their clients, to provide healing and transformation. In my model, this source of universal compassion is associated with the oneness aspect of the continuum. But I recognize that as soon as we try to describe it we have missed it. So I bask in the mystery of the unknowable and the divine.

(Footnotes)

1 http://www.shamanism.org Web site has full calendar of workshops offered across the globe.

2 Harner, Michael; The Way of the Shaman; Harper and Row, 1980 and 1990, page 21

Carla Person is a shamanic practitioner in Veneta, Oregon, who has worked with the spirits for over 15 years to help people and animals become well and whole. She practices core shamanism, using ancient healing techniques that are common to many cultures and compatible with our modern world.

She has pioneered a simple method for telepathic-style animal communication based in shamanic practices, which she teaches in workshops across the country. Carla is happy to help people, but the focus of her work is with animals. All sorts of domestic and wild animals have been recipients of her spirit allies' gracious healing power.

While Carla has studied with many important humans, including completing the most advanced training with Michael Harner and the Foundation for Shamanic Studies, her true teachers are spirits who have deep compassion for incarnate beings' pain and suffering. When a guardian asks Carla to help a troubled animal with a mysterious malady, it is the spirits' wisdom that cracks the case, and their healing power that offers relief. Carla is the conduit, guiding the process through her intention and deep experience in this work.

Carla regularly offers workshops at her farm near Eugene, Oregon, and is available for teaching in other locations. For those who like to learn at home, or at their own pace, she has created an instructional DVD of her introductory workshop called *Speak to My Heart: Carla Person's Step By Step Method for Shamanic Animal Communication* (Coccora Press 2003)

For more information on Carla's work, to schedule a session for your animal or yourself, and to learn about attending or hosting a workshop please see Carla's website, www.spirithealer.com

147

How do your animals truly feel?
What do they really want?

Reclaim your innate ability to speak with animals, uncovering their deepest desires.

Carla Person's Step-by-Step Method for Shamanic Animal Communication

Speak to My Heart!

Learn to talk with your animals using the ancient techniques of shamanism

Speak to My Heart! is the first DVD to teach Animal Communication using the Shamanic Method. Pioneered by Carla Person, these step-by-step instructions teach you to
• enter the shamanic world of spirits
• meet your personal power animal
• communicate with living animals
• gain deeper understanding of your animal's feelings

Learning to talk with animals is easy using the Shamanic Method – the way earth's original peoples communicate with other beings. Clear instructions are intermixed with workshop footage for a rich learning experience.

$34.95 Retail ISBN 0-9744145-1-4
(Also available on VHS ISBN 0-9744145-2-2)

For ordering retail and wholesale: www.coccorapress.com
Coccora Press, PO Box 679, Veneta OR 97487
or call 541-935-4996

Speak to My Heart!

Retail orders include free shipping and money back guarantee.